GOD, I LISTENED TOO

To: Ajaya Woods 10-23-2021

Blessings

GOD, I LISTENED TOO

By
La-Doris McClaney

MCCLANEY MEDIA

God, I Listened Too
Autobiography
ISBN: 9780578923390

Jacket Portrait, Photos by Allison Johnson at lawgraphics.com and
Sherre Titus. Portrait by Will Utley at willutley.com

FIRST EDITION

Copyright © 2021 by Dr. La-Doris McClaney
First Printing 2021

Printed in the United States of America.
Library of Congress Cataloging in Publication Data on file.

Published by
McClaney Media
Los Angeles, California

McClaneymedia.com

INSPIRATION

My international students have become part of my family. They started calling me "Mommy" almost immediately after their arrival. I nurture, love, and encourage them to be their best selves, and in turn, they have filled my life with joy, a tremendous amount of laughter, and now, they are the inspiration for this book. *God, I Listened Too* would not be possible without Amr Shahat and Wadie Chalgham, two of my "sons." These men are the reason I've chosen to write my memoirs. Their daily insistence that I sit in front of my computer and revisit parts of my past was relentless. They challenged me, questioned me, and gave me the push I needed to place the story of my life on these pages. Even though I have been asked for many years by many people to write my memoirs, until Amr, Wadie, and I were in Covid-19 quarantine in March 2020, I had no desire to do so.

Amr and Wadie, thank you for being the wind in my sails. It is because of you that I am sharing my complex and beautiful life story with the world.

Love, Mommy

Amr Khalaf Shahat, PhD
Archaeology

Wadie Chalgham, PhD
Mechanical Engineering

Special thanks to
Shelbi M. Walker, J.D.
for your skill with the quill
and
Sherre Titus
for your love of Common Wealth

DEDICATION

To my Almighty God,
my parents, and my sister.

TABLE OF CONTENTS

"The Lord is my shepherd; I shall not want.

He maketh me to lie down in green pastures:
He leadeth me beside the still waters.

He restoreth my soul: He leadeth me in the paths of righteousness for
His name's sake.

Yea, though I walk through the valley of the shadow of death, I will fear no
evil: for thou art with me; thy rod and thy staff they comfort me.

Thou preparest a table before me in the presence of mine enemies:
thou anointest my head with oil; my cup runneth over.

Surely goodness and mercy shall follow me all the days of my life:
and I will dwell in the house of the Lord forever."

Psalm 23

FOREWORD

I first met Dr. McClaney at church. My husband Sam, our daughter Zoe and I had recently moved to the Los Angeles area and we had been attending various churches to find a church home. I was taken by the spirited congregation and charismatic minister, Bishop Charles E. Blake, Sr., at West Angeles Church and so I kept returning each Sunday. I must admit that I noticed this very well dressed and stately woman with the wide smile each time I attended service. There was just something about her which commanded your attention. Maybe it was how she walked with her head held high in confidence, always dressed for church in the latest designer ensemble.

We were finally introduced by Doretha Leflore, one of the ushers with whom I had become friendly. "LaTanya, this is Dr. La-Doris McClaney, a leading member of our church. La-Doris, this is LaTanya Jackson. She is married to the actor, Samuel L. Jackson and they just moved here from New York." I guess Doretha thought that a bit of Hollywood information lifted me in the art of the introduction. When Dr. McClaney spoke, her voice reminded me of the women oratorical speakers, with their articulate, rolling vocals, whom I'd grown up listening to in Atlanta, Georgia. Her smile and tone welcomed me, as she offered her help with what needs I might have, since I was new to California. It didn't take long before I was totally in awe of this obviously prosperous Black woman, who was quick to let me know that she needed nothing from me and that she was possibly more impressed with me than the fame of my husband — at least that is how I took it.

With each succeeding Sunday, we grew closer. Our conversations of the historical significance of the church in our lives and how God helps us to succeed and bear the burdens of our responsibilities, the importance of taking care of our health by going to wellness centers and creating nutritional pathways for that health, the importance ofphilanthropy and helping our fellow man, of being a truthful person of your word knowing how to be a good friend, being civic minded and participating in the political process affecting our communities, these were topics of interest which drew me closer to her and made her my new Shero.

She was always somewhere doing something, whether presiding over the Links, Incorporated, or receiving an award from Los Angeles City Council, or getting another honorary degree to add to the over 500 other awards she has received. She became my friend in 1992 and by 2021 had become my Big Sister.

She is a woman to be emulatedand many years agoLa-Doris shared her beginnings with me by giving me her Mother's autobiography, *God, I Listened*, which explained to me so much about where La-Doris-got her drive to achieve and be accomplished through the severest of adversities which her Mother faced. To be at a point in her life when she is willing to share how she has been able to reach heights which have put her at the top of the game of life, dressed in jewels and designer chic, is a significant testimony which we all can find extraordinary. Dr. La-Doris McClaney is the real deal and I love her.

LaTanya Richardson Jackson
Actress, Producer, Director

INTRODUCTION

Nestled between a wooden shack with no electricity or running water, and a multi-million-dollar mansion situated next door to movie stars, is a life story built on hard work, grit, and commitment. This life, in all its complexity and beauty, is my life. It began humbly with me, my sister, and my parents having a collective desire to enjoy the abundance promised to us by the Creator. A life better from the one from which we descended. One where we could build upon a foundation of service, sacrifice, and education and grow a lasting legacy.

After losing my sister and my Mother, I continued this journey and kept the McClaney legacy of giving countless financial gifts to support education, mental health, the American Lung Association, the American Cancer Society and incalculable in-kind work to keep the dreams of my family alive. This commitment has allowed me to open my home in Holmby Hills to international students seeking higher education and hosting foster children at my estate in Las Vegas.

By no means is this memoir designed to be an exploration or celebration of all my achievements. Rather, it should serve as inspiration to those whose eyes and minds are filled with its pages, that life is what you make it. Nothing is ever obtained without hard work, strong faith, and intentionally seeking more knowledge. My prayer is that through my life story you will see your own possibilities and begin to get into the flow of God's plan for you. It begins with a step, a seed, and an open ear to listen.

I have been many places and shared the table with many dignitaries including President Gerald Ford, beloved former Mayor of Los Angeles, Tom Bradley, and the Royal families in the United Arab

Emirates. Though these notable people are revered and celebrated, not one of them was as powerful or impactful in my life than Eula McClaney - my Mother. Who would have imagined that a poor, Black, uneducated woman would have had the foresight and tenacity to enter into the world of real estate in a time when women were forbidden to have a store charge card without their husband's permission and signature?She was a trailblazer and my greatest inspiration. It is because of her that I am.

She gave birth to me and with every push thereafter, I was thrust into a new more challenging adventure. She explained that my role in the family was to expand our real estate empire which I have done for more than 50 years. Unlike many people who lose what they inherit within weeks or months after a death, I was committed to take good care of what she left in my charge. She was calculated and insisted that I be part of the establishment of our business to truly understand the growth of our wealth. My greatest joy, however, is not the accumulation of things, but rather giving to those in need. I continue to give to organizations that focus on the health and education of economically disadvantaged communities. Not only have I sustained what we built as a family, but I have also added to it and paved new ways for scores of marginalized people in Los Angeles, Las Vegas, and beyond. From the outside looking in, it would appear that I have lived a very privileged life. The fact is that I worked very hard to maintain the mandate from my Mother - keep the family business going.

I am writing my life story because I have been encouraged by so many people to do so. After my Mother wrote her memoirs, *God I Listened*, I decided that her legacy was to continue through me, and her story would have a continuing and lasting postscript. You will find that these pages don't hold a magic spell or even a solution to your problems. Rather, a story of what it took for me to dream the impossible, and ultimately live it. As with many people, the quarantine of 2020 because of the Covid-19 pandemic gave me enough personal pause to reflect on what was most important to me, how I can be a better servant of God, and what I wanted to be remembered for. I began to reflect on my life and the wisdom I accumulated to inspire future generations. Thankfully Wadie and Amr, two of the international students who were both working on their respective Doctoral studies at the University of California, Los Angeles (UCLA), who have been with me for 4-years, inspired and encouraged me to write. Those two young men are the reason that this book is resting in your hands. Amr was awakened one night from a deep sleep. He had a dream. My Mother appeared to him and told him to tell me to write my memoirs. At first, I thought he had gone mad, but upon reflection, I decided that my life had meaning, and my story needed to be told. The three of us set out to do just that.

People who know me or know of me likely believe that I was born with a silver spoon in my mouth, on the contrary. In fact, there were times when there were no spoons at all. They believe that the material possessions that I have are what I value most. Mansions, expensive cars, and designer clothes don't define me as a person. They are mere manifestations of hard work, good money management, and sound investments. The heart of who I am as a woman and a child of God is what most people can't see with the naked eye. It is the Grace of God in my life and the voice that I listen to so that I may fulfill His greater purpose through me. Yes, *God, I Listened Too*. Rest in the knowledge that you too can attune your ear to Him and discover your place in His greater, most miraculous, Divine Will.

If you take only one thing away after reading my memoirs I pray that what moves you most is that no matter where you come from or what your current position is in the world, God has a dream for you that is bigger than you can imagine. Your abundant life isn't determined by the opulence of your home or the size of your bank account. The Abundant Life promised to you starts with how much you love, give to, and serve your fellow man. And if you find yourself in desperation, want, or despair, remember that weeping may endure for a night, but joy cometh in the morning. Wake up, rise, and live.

La-Doris

PART I

Troy, Alabama

My Family

They named me La-Doris. I never understood how Georgia Mae, my Mother's sister, came up with my name. It always seemed a bit exotic for a girl who was born in Troy, Alabama. It was an unconventional name given to me, a baby girl, on June 19, 1938. My Mother's labor started and stopped in the backwoods of Troy, Alabama, Pike County.

I came into the world in my grandparent's one-bedroom shack surrounded by family. This home, that was the foyer of my beginnings, was humble. Small, dark, but immaculate. No matter where we lived, my Mother always maintained an impeccable space for us to call home. Even with very little finances, she was able to create a beautiful space complete with tablecloths made from old bed sheets, and small glass trinkets that could rival any Baccarat figure today. She had an eye for interior design, even in Troy. She would create her own design theories and then put them into action on a fixed income. She even refinished the warped wood floors by sanding them to a mirrored smoothness and ebony soaked shine. Legend has it, that as I was entering the world from my Mother's body, those wooden floor slats almost received me first. There were gaps in our wood floors which were the perfect size for my tiny newborn frame to slip through onto the dirt floor beneath. The quick thinking and steady hands of the midwife prevented my fall. She caught me and immediately placed me in the arms of my beloved Mother where she held me close. There I lay on her bosom, surely inhaling the warmth and love of each of her deep breaths. She, in her steady tone, thanked God for my safe

1

arrival and placed a blessing upon my head, "For this child, I prayed. Thank you, Lord." With that, my ear was open to listen to Him in my life, for my entire life.

I was a small, delicate baby with dainty features. At all of 6 pounds, my cries were slight, but strong enough to beckon the eager ears of my parents. The night that I came into the world, my grandfather, who wasn't particularly soft in his countenance or actively involved in my Mother's pregnancy, rushed to the midwife to ensure her arrival before my birth. He needed to be needed, and he was. When he fled in the night in search of the midwife, he rode his beautiful chestnut brown horse. The horse was as arrogant and stately as my grandfather. That horse, being feverishly ridden to the house of the community midwife, was all the help my grandfather could muster as I was making my grand entrance into the world.

At the time of my birth, my parents Eula (Bie) Hendrick McClaney and Burnish (Bernie) McClaney, were impoverished. They lived in a dilapidated wooden shack with enough holes in the tin roof where the night sky was visible to their eyes as they lay in their bed or collect rainwater for cleaning or drinking after a hard Alabama spring storm. As for furnishings, there was one bed and one table flanked by two wooden chairs. The weathered walls were rough and dark with an oxidized patina. The kitchen, as with most homes, was the heart of the house. A small sink, an icebox, and a wood stove was the source of all our meals. Daily, that wood stove served as a stage for a culinary masterpiece. A large cast iron pot would teeter on the burners as the simmering dish that my Mother had created from any scraps of meat and vegetables that she could muster came to a raging boil. Behind it, a fragrant coffee can filled with the oily remnants of the meal from the night before or the bacon drippings that were added after breakfast in the morning. That rich oil was used for everything from cooking, to greasing scalps, to moisturizing the skin of her dry knees. They didn't have much, but they had food and family. My parents eeked out a living as sharecroppers. Day after day they labored in the hot Alabama sun, plowing, and tilling the soil, planting, and picking cotton to support me and my sister Burnie who was three years older than I. My parents performed back-breaking work that offered mediocre pay and no hope for the future. My parents worked to survive. They came home bone tired after hours of picking cotton. Their clothes were soiled from the mix of dirt and sweat. Their shoes bore holes and scuff marks serving as the only remaining memory of leather that had been torn from the vamp. They worked sun-up to sundown with little to no breaks in between, as did most of the adults in Troy.

Troy, the place of my birth, was a small segregated town with a population of just over 7,000 people. It was the quintessential segregated South; White people lived on one side of town and Blacks on the other. If Mississippi was the Heart of the Jim Crow South, then Troy was its main artery, pumping the thick red blood of hate into the body of our country. The ugly stench of racism permeated the brick streets and historic buildings. Though there were many threats of racism and violence aimed at Black people, it was the only life my parents knew. This era in this city represented everything about racism in this country. What my people had to endure just to survive is unimaginable. I marvel at the level of pure restraint and deference that my parents and grandparents must have exercised daily just to survive.

My maternal grandparents, Joe Frank Hendrick and Joanna Holt Hendrick were from Orion, Alabama, a small town just 15 miles from Troy. They raised my Mother and her siblings in poverty and want of resources. They had a strong unyielding faith in God and a complete belief in His Biblical promises. My paternal grandfather, Hillard McClaney was from Troy, Alabama. My grandmother had died before they married.

My Mother's upbringing was traditional. Her Father, my grand-father, was a hard man who worked my Mother like an animal in the fields. My grandmother was a quiet, meek, timid woman who endured decades of overbearing behavior from my grandfather. My Mother and her siblings often wondered why their Mother tolerated his hard-ness. He wasn't abusive, but his antics would often send shockwaves throughout their home. My Mother would tell us how hard she had to work in the fields along with her two brothers. She matched their efforts pound for pound, working alongside them without complaint. She and her brothers were very close. Working side-by-side every day for decades will do that to you. Her life didn't afford much oppor-tunity to have a social life, so her brothers became her best friends.

Hers was a complicated life peppered with loss and grief. Her eldest brother Joe Frank, Jr. (Bae) died when he was 21 years old. His death was shrouded in mystery that remains to this day. It devastated my Mother. A piece of her died when he died, and she was never the same. She had a sister named Georgia Mae whom she loved dearly even though they were not treated the same as children. Georgia Mae was the self-proclaimed and evident apple of her parent's eye; my Mother was the stem. Georgia Mae was special. She was treated as though she was delicate and fragile. Her wrongs were always right, and her rights were always perfect. There was little she could do to cause a stir in the hearts of my grandparents. My Mother's sister was not permitted to attend the same school, nor work in the fields like she and her brothers Jimmie Lee and Tommy Lee. She never worked the fields. Instead, Georgia Mae spent her days in the kitchen cooking for the family or enjoying some leisure activity while my Mother matched physical wits with her brothers as they tended to the fields.

As a child, my Mother and her brothers walked four miles one way to school while Georgia Mae was sent away to a boarding school.

My Mother often recounted that she felt like she was treated like the stepsister in a fairytale. Her sister was prized and privileged, while she and her brothers were treated in a very different way. My Mother was the proverbial Cinderella as a child.

Georgia Mae would return from boarding school with stories of fanciful experiences that my Mother could only dream of. Georgia Mae knew of her privilege and because of it, she stayed home to cook while my Mother and her brothers worked in the fields with their parents. Jimmie Lee and Tommy Lee loved each other but their love was rarely expressed. There was really no room for relationship building or folly. They were workers and their bond, along with my Mother's to them, was forged in the Alabama soil and with every prick of the cotton bristles. Georgia Mae was an outstanding cook and her hand bore no scars from fieldwork. Her contribution to the family was her sumptuous meals and sparkling personality. The family could hardly wait to come in from the field after a long, hard day just to taste Georgia Mae's cooking. They knew they were in for a treat.

My maternal grandmother, Joanna Holt, was a shy, timid, quiet woman who had lost her mother at an early age and was raised by her Father, Tom. She could barely muster a smile and never made eye contact with anyone. Her head was always hung as low as the branches of a willow tree. My Mother loved her, but secretly I think she resented the fact that her mother never stood up for herself. She even froze like a frightened doe at the thought of having to communicate with anyone. In those days, many women were seen and not heard, and my grandmother was no exception to that rule. Her role as wife and Mother were clearly defined and her voice, in those days, was veiled by her husband. His way was the only way. In spite of that, she was sweet and gentle and never caused a stir even though she had no rights and no voice.

My grandmother's brother was a preacher who ruled with a switch and a Bible. He believed in Jesus and judgement, and one didn't trump the other. He had no softness in him. My grandfather was a different sort of person. I inherited some of his characteristics. He was the man of his house. He made no apologies for his beliefs or actions, whether he was right or wrong and according to my Mother, he was usually wrong. He was the impetus for her to become the woman that she was.

Hard Work

Fields of puffy white cotton were the morning glories for my parents. They awakened every day before the sun to tend acres and acres of these demanding, unforgiving crops. Cotton was a year-round boss. They would start preparing the ground and planting sometime in March and await the harvest in June. During the growing period, they were in constant communication with the crop. Cotton is complicated. The softness of the flower is juxtaposed to the sharpness of its thorns. Picking and tending to it requires laser focus and a skilled and steady hand. It is almost an art to pick cotton. Bags and bags every day, making sure the fluff was ripe and smooth to the touch. A day too late and the cotton crumbled in hand, one day too early, and the cotton is no good. They were experts in understanding the blossom and her delicate and temperamental nature.

My parents didn't own the land that they tended. They rented the field to grow their crops. The "boss man," Mr. Murphy, would lend them just enough money to run their crop for the year, leaving only pennies for extra supplies or extravagant benefits like new shoes or clothing. During the season, they would often pick fifteen-hundred pounds of cotton before they could go to the cotton gin to have it baled.

When it was cotton-picking time, they would pick the cotton and take it to the gin mill. The mill would thrust the seed from the cotton and then it would be baled. Once the seeds were removed and the cotton baled, they would be left with five hundred pounds of lint or plain cotton, which would be ready to be put on the market. They would also have cotton seeds which was used for the next planting season. Nothing was wasted, in the cotton mill or in our home. Everything had a purpose. Everything, no matter how insignificant, could be used again and again, to benefit the family.

In addition to cotton, my parents had corn and other crops to tend. They planted items that were meal staples in our home and feed for the livestock. Cotton, however, was the king that dominated their lives and the monies they yielded from it secured our place in poverty and want. Cotton, they soon learned, was a jealous mistress. It occupied most of their time and offered no sustainable long-term benefit.

They had to make provisions for their own food. The hogs mostly ate corn in the wintertime. They also raised my favorite foods, black-eyed peas, and sweet potatoes. During the fruit seasons, they would trespass on the neighboring farm and pick blueberries and blackberries, risking pricks to their already marred hands from the thorns on the blackberries. Sometimes they would have to walk miles to find them. The magic that my Mother and her sister did with those meager ingredients would put any chef to shame. Those meals were spectacular. Smoked meat, seasoned corn, and greens deserved a Michelin star. They worked hard on their farm and the farm of my grandparents. Alongside one another; male and female, old and young. My family didn't know it at the time, but with each seed planted in the ground, a seed was being planted in the soul of my parents. The harvest would come years later, and a bumper crop would emerge.

Tending to the field left little time for recreation or entertainment. My Mother would often reminisce about the good times in her life on the farm when they killed their beef and hogs and dressed the meat. When it was time to kill the hogs, my grandfather would get his twenty-two-caliber rifle that would shoot two tiny bullets. I can still hear the sound as the shots rang out. My grandfather would post up with focused aim. He watched as a hog waddled around the pen. Oblivious to his fate, the hog moved with a snail's pace due to his rotund size. Patiently, my grandfather waited until the hog was in the perfect position. He set his aim between the hog's eyes and then, "Pow." They would then hang the hog up on a post and cut it from neck to stomach. They ate everything that came from the hog.

The smokehouse was in the backyard. They made the fire from hickory wood cut from the trees that were adjacent to the field. All the meat would be put into the smokehouse and hung up for 4 to 5 days. The smoke that billowed from that smoker was like a welcome mat to the neighbors. My Mother enjoyed seeing her parents sharing the meat with other families in the county. There was a sense of community among all the families. The hog served as a means to bring people together and feed those that had little to eat. All winter, the community and our family would sup and survive off the hanging meat in the smokehouse. Even though they had little, they shared everything with their neighbors. In this time, to survive, you had to rely upon the village of people around you. Selflessness was a means of survival. Without it, you could not survive.

My Mother was short, heavy set and always had shoulder length hair. I thought that she was beautiful, but she always described herself as average looking. She had an infectious, almost hypnotic laugh. You felt her joy emanate through the room when she caught something funny enough in her soul. She would burst out in laughter and her smile could light an entire room. She quipped that the only reason she was heavy was because she loved to eat. When she was a child, her parents took her to the circus. The family couldn't afford to watch the show, so they would pack a lunch and stand outside as the animals were paraded into the tent. On one occasion, my grandmother allowed my Mother to hold the lunch pail filled with pig feet sandwiches and sweet potato pie for her and her brothers. This was a high honor since it was the only meal that she and her brothers would have after the parade of animals. After the last elephant entered the tent, my grandmother turned to my Mother and asked for the lunch pail. By that time, everyone was famished. When my Mother handed over the pail, it was completely empty. My Mother had eaten EVERYTHING! Her love of food was never more evident. Her family, hungry and mad, watched my Mother, with a full belly, waddle back home. She often shared that sentiment and it was always followed by her bold, beautiful, full laugh.

Georgia Mae, her sister, was tall, slim, pretty with long beautiful hair. Hers was a beauty that many envied and, at times, attempted to imitate. She was a beautiful woman. She became smitten by a tall handsome man named Malakai. They dated for a while and decided to run away and get married without her parent's permission. She told my Mother because she knew that my Mother wasn't going to violate her trust. My Mother was devastated when Georgia Mae eloped. My Mother was left with the secret of the forbidden marriage and the loss of her sister. Holding that secret would stay with her for years. And she never chose to divulge what she knew. My grandfather would threaten to whip my Mother because he felt she knew that Georgia Mae was leaving. My Mother took aim on holding Georgia Mae's secret much like my grandfather did when he shot the hogs. Unwavering, unflinching, laser focused on what she decided to do for her sister. Patiently, she waited and remained quiet. Any motion to the contrary would be detrimental to her and her sister.

When Mom finally had an opportunity to get her hair done and wear a new dress, she felt beautiful because she had always worn Georgia Mae's hand me downs. I often wondered how my portly Mother wore the clothes that were purchased for her slender sister. I discovered that back then, women wore sack dresses. These dresses lacked shape and true size so a sack dress was a one-size-fits-all frock! Georgia Mae knew that her sister was not treated the same. She was burdened by the idea that she was special, and my Mother wasn't. They were sisters and to my Mother, Georgia Mae was a window into the possibilities of life. My Mother often lay awake dreaming of a life outside of the fields of Troy. She dreamed of having beautiful things and privilege. Many times, when Georgia Mae was given money to buy hats and dresses, she always saw fit to purchase something for my Mother. She wanted so desperately to be seen as a woman like Georgia Mae, instead of as a workhorse in the fields. My Mother was a feminine woman who wasn't allowed to be. Her Father saw her as a worker, not as a woman. Her role was set in stone and her place was in the field. Even though Georgia Mae was privileged and never permitted to work in the way my Mother did, she loved her. She loved her sister and never resented her. Their love was deep, whole, and lasting.

Decades later, in the last five years of her life, Georgia Mae came to live with my Mother. My Mother took excellent care of her. By this time, my Mother was living in California. Georgia Mae had first gone to the San Fernando Valley to live with her daughter. She wanted to stay with my Mother because she missed her sister, her Mother, and her sisters cooking. Georgia Mae had had a hard life plagued by alcoholism and failed relationships. My Mother graciously allowed Georgia Mae to live with us under one condition - she was forbidden from drinking. Georgia Mae complied and never took another drink. She, with all her beauty and talent in the kitchen, had done little in her life. Her childhood privilege and non-existent work ethic funneled into her adult life. Adult behavior is born in childhood and because she wasn't forced to work, nor was she made to believe that she should work, she only did so when she had to in childhood and adulthood. What Georgia Mae did, however, was care for and love her sister.

My Mother said she would always be grateful for the way Georgia Mae looked out for her when she was unable to take care of herself. She loved Georgia Mae so much and was grateful that she was in the position to now, take care of her sister. Before Georgia Mae passed, I would watch the two sisters sit and chat about their lives together. They held precious secrets between them. The love that they shared was priceless. To be able to sit and watch the two of them holding hands and laughing would bring tears to your eyes. Mother was never jealous of Georgia Mae, and Georgia Mae fully understood her privileged position. They often talked about how, even amongst their parents, the sins of colorism and privilege wafted through the air like the smoke from the smokehouse. If my Mother were a lesser woman, she would have choked on the billows of favoritism, but neither ever consumed its ugliness.

Parents' Relationship

My Mother met my Daddy, Bernard Albert McClaney, at her grandmother's church, Pleasant Grove Baptist Church in Troy, Alabama. My Father was a tall handsome man. His chiseled chin and sculpted nose looked like they had been handcrafted out of marble by a Greek artist. He was charming and kind. My Father was a hard worker and could stand up to any adversity, except his Father. He had been raised in a family where my grandfather dominated everything, even the town where they lived. My Father was the unfortunate by-product of years and years of beratement by his Father. He was always seeking peace and didn't tolerate any form of confrontation. He was a very content man. He had an aversion to risk, and he kept life expectations practical and steady. He met my Mother and he didn't know at the time, but steady was about to marry a tornado.

The church has always been a constant in my family. There was rarely a fourth Sunday that went by that we weren't in full worship, dressed in our Sunday best and singing songs of praise and promise. Every measure of entertainment in Troy centered around the church. God, work, and food were the trinity of Troy. My parents meeting at church wasn't an anomaly. Most relationships, at that time, began with meeting in church. I'm not sure who was smitten first, but I know that they fell in love that day. They cultivated their relationship by writing letters to each other. Mother's address was simple; *Eula Hendrick Route #3, Troy, Alabama.* My Father committed that address to memory when he first heard it. To send a letter at that time would cost two cents. They exchanged letters and expressed their love for one another. Dates were rare because work came first.

When Mom told her Father that Bernie wanted to be her boyfriend, he didn't object. My Father came from a highly respected family in Alabama. The family owned over 100 acres of land. My paternal grandfather was both revered and feared. Jim Crow was a season in time when Black people were being beaten or killed just for being Black. The times offered little to no opportunity for Black people. My grandfather would traverse his vast land on horseback with a rifle strapped to his back. He was the king of his kingdom and he dared anyone to cross his path. He had a team of horses, several heads of cattle, hogs, and children that he worked into submission. He was a hard man, who worked his children even harder.

My Father lived 15 miles away from my Mother and they only saw each other once a month. Work prevented courtship and those chance meetings at church were the only opportunity for them to exchange loving looks. While Georgia Mae was dating feverishly at boarding school and eloping at will, my Mother was hard pressed to see my Father at all. Mother had no intention of running off and getting married without her parents knowing because she knew how much Georgia Mae's actions had hurt them. My Mother forwent her footloose and fancy-free dreams to adhere to the tenets that she had been taught - faith, family, and doing what was right. Though she was eager to get from under the thumb of her Father and his demands for her to work so hard, she stayed until her Father allowed for her to marry. She always said that she wanted to leave her parent's house the right way just in case she ever had to come back she could do so.

Her Father liked Bernie, but he told people that he hated to see my Mother leave because she was one of the best workers he had. My Mother wasn't surprised because she knew she was just a workhorse for him. She was never his daughter. She was only a worker. Her Father finally gave in and gave her permission to marry my Dad. He was not at all happy to see her leave. He gave her a few things to take with her such as a trunk, iron-framed bed, box springs, and a mattress. As a bride, she only had a few things to take with her. She married Dad in the middle of the Depression. She had managed to save $20 to purchase her wedding dress, shoes, stockings, and a few extra items. She even bought a hat for the day. My Mother had a large head and the hat didn't fit at all. Decades later, she hired a milliner to come to our home to size her head and create custom hats that she would wear on occasion. She earned the extra money teaching school to some of the other children in the county. Amazingly, she did this with only a sixth-grade education. As a child, she went to school for a short period of time, but she had a thirst for learning. She knew that education was the key to the kingdom.

My parents married in 1933 and moved into a house behind my paternal grandfather. That home was 15 miles north of Troy, near Orion. If Troy was the country, steeped in Southern tradition and racism; Bullock County was the fire that heated the pot of segregation, division, and racial tension. This was the first time that my Mother was away from her parents. She was 22.

Mom and Dad sharecropped on Dad McClaney's land. The house stood on rickety stilts and the slats that formed the walls were gapped and splintered. At any given moment a strong wind could have blown the house down around them. My Mother, even in this house, was determined to make a home for her husband. It consisted of two rooms, a kitchen, bedroom, and a porch. Their facilities were an outhouse. They had no electricity and no indoor plumbing. The house was careworn, but it was theirs. Dad McClaney had built this house for his Mother-in-law and she lived there until she died. There were no window treatments and my Mother always hated that. Anyone could walk by and look straight into the house. At some point, she collected enough money to purchase window coverings for the tiny windows that dotted the house. She was proud to put up those curtains for privacy and to make the house look more attractive. Eventually, she bought bed sheets to match. Even then, when money wasn't available for such extravagance as curtains, my Mother was determined to make our house a home. After working hard in the field and saving a little money they began to purchase a few items. My parents took pride in purchasing small trinkets such as small cigar boxes and intricately painted glass vases to create the illusion of wealth and prestige.

My Mother and my paternal grandfather had a remarkable relationship. There was something about how they interacted with one another that I think may have caused irreparable damage to my Father's relationship with his father. My Mother had a way with her Father-in-law that my Father just could never obtain. My paternal grandfather was a wonderful man in many ways. My Mother learned that he was aggressive, strong minded, and strong willed. My Father characterized him as something other than those things. He was a scary man with a reputation of getting whatever he wanted. He personally owned over 100 acres of land in Alabama. He was admired and feared by both Black and White people and when he rode up on his steed over his empire, he did so with a shotgun on his back. He was no one to fool with.

Dad McClaney was a great influence on my Mother's life because of his strength and ability to get things accomplished during these segregated and trying times. Even though times were difficult, my grandfather was able to do the impossible. He was less of a Father and more of an employer to his children. My Father never was able to see his soft side. In fact, I don't believe one ever even existed in my grandfather. Though he was quite accomplished in his business life, his personal life suffered. His children would never know his heart. They learned that his love was conditioned on their ability to tend to the fields and to increase his income. Their childhood was marred with just utilitarianism. No joy. No carefreeness. Just work.

After my parents married, my Mother would spend quite a bit of time with my paternal grandfather. Likely more so than my Father even. My Mother was an inquisitive person who often questioned those who were successful to understand how they got where they were. Her Father-in-law was no different. My Mother set her sights on understanding how he had obtained so much wealth and so much property during a time when Black men were often marginalized and forbidden from owning land. My grandfather had an old trunk where he kept his deeds. During the day, he would often allow my Mother to read them. She asked questions and always wanted to know the ins and outs of property ownership. She knew that ownership meant freedom and that freedom meant choice. Secretly, I believe my Father was unhappy about her inquisitiveness. My Father resented her because she was able to communicate in a way with his Father that he could not. During that time, women were to be seen and not heard, but my Mother was different. She always wanted a different life for her and my Father and for us girls. She was so impressed with seeing his name on those deeds. She dreamed that one day her name would appear on a deed too.

My Birth Story

My Mother loved being a wife and a Mother. She was a strong smart woman who believed in the institution of the nuclear family. She spent her days ensuring that her husband and her children were well taken care of, loved, and supported in every way. Prior to my birth, my parents got into some sort of disagreement. The details are unclear, but the story remains. Whatever happened in that evening, angered my Mother to such an extent, that she, eight and a half months pregnant with me, packed up my older sister and a bag and preceded to traverse the Alabama woods in search of her parent's home. She left under the dark of night to escape their argument. The sky was black as coal, with the stars shining like diamonds above her head. My sister, just shy of three years old, was double stepping behind her as she huffed and puffed through the thickets and the dampness of the Alabama woods. Every so often, she would hear the rustling of wildlife in the distance, or an unfamiliar sound just ahead. She was undeterred, unafraid, and hell bent on getting to her parent's house. A lesser woman would have stopped, turned around, and gone back home. But not my Mother. When she made a decision, she stuck with it no matter how hard the road may have been.

She finally stopped at a house on the side of the road and asked the people to let her ride one of their horses to her parent's home. The family was bewildered that someone was at the door, least of which a heavily pregnant woman and her toddler. They obliged and allowed her to ride their horse the rest of the way to her parent's home. Even though the subject of the argument is unknown, you must be pretty mad to be eight and a half months pregnant, walk miles to an unknown home, and then hitch a ride on an unfamiliar horse with your toddler. I often wonder if my fight and determination came that night as my Mother traversed those woods. As she inhaled, I inhaled. As she fought through the thickets and the animals and the waste and the darkness, I did so too, in utero, with her. I wonder if that's where it all began for me. The next day, my Father arrived at my grandparent's home. His countenance was sheepish and shocked. He couldn't believe that my Mom walked 15 miles in the dark, borrowed a horse, and planted herself at their home, all because of an argument. I think my Father took the horse back as a way of making amends to my Mother.

In the months following my birth, my Mom became convinced that the best thing for my Father, her children, and herself, would be to leave Alabama and go live in the North. She was determined to live anywhere north of the Mason-Dixon Line. She had never been anywhere but Troy. She had never seen any other place, but she knew that more was possible. My Mother wanted Burnie and I to have a better life than she and Dad had in Alabama. She couldn't visualize Burnie and I working in the fields picking cotton and doing all the hard labor that she and my Father endured. She wasn't at all concerned where we lived, so long as it wasn't in the South. Dad was not hard to convince because he was also tired of the hard work in the hot fields of Alabama and he wanted to escape from his Father's tight, unyielding grip. Whatever was on the other side of the Mason-Dixon Line had to be better than Troy.

He didn't like the fact that his father was so hard on his children working them like animals. Now he was trying to figure out where to go. Since he was apprehensive to go anywhere else where there was no family, he decided that he would go to Pittsburgh, Pennsylvania where he had some distant relatives and he would feel safe because it was his first time out of the South. He hated to leave my Mother, Burnie, and me but he knew he needed to find employment and a place for us to stay when we joined him. It was four months before he fetched for us.

PART II

Pittsburgh, Pennsylvania

Early Life in Pittsburgh

My Mother left Alabama in 1940 to join my Father who had left four months prior. Leaving Alabama that day was one of the most important days of her life. In fact, it changed the entire trajectory of her existence. It was the seed of success being planted deep into the Alabama soil, only to flourish in Pittsburgh, Pennsylvania, and ultimately Los Angeles, California.

My Mother only knew Alabama. For her entire life, she lived, worked, married, and had children there. It was all she knew. That day, she was terrified at the idea of leaving all that she had ever known. But terror did not trump her desire to have a better life for herself and her family. The night before she left, she could barely eat or sleep. The day that we were to depart the South, she gathered up my sister and I, with all of our bags and toys, to board a train from Montgomery to Pittsburgh. My Mother's bravery is unfathomable. There she was, a short, stout Black woman toting her two daughters into an unknown world all alone. The only consolation was that she didn't have much to carry. She didn't have much at all. She brought a few dresses for Burnie, and some powdered milk for me, for the long train ride. Her cousin sent a trunk full of items that would make it to Pittsburgh before we arrived.

She carried a purse with a little money in case of an emergency. It was less than $50.00. This is a woman who'd never left a 30-mile radius, and there she was, on a train, with two children anticipating the transfer of trains to Cincinnati. The entire time she traveled from

Cincinnati to Pittsburgh, she thought about how she would manage two children on a train, and transfer in a city that she'd never seen or been to before. In fact, I'm not quite sure she even knew how to spell C-i-n-c-i-n-n-a-t-i. The same woman who fearlessly traversed the Alabama woods while pregnant, shook with fear at the prospect of transferring trains in Cincinnati. She was so worried that she would miss the train and feared the response she may receive by asking others for assistance. She soon found out that her inquisitive nature would serve her well in situations unknown to her. She asked several people how and where the transfer would occur. They obliged, and she boarded the proper train with Burnie and me in tow. After asking 100 times if she was on the right train, she heard the conductor say, "All Aboard to Pittsburgh, Pennsylvania." She couldn't wait to get on the train and find a seat and settle down. She was so excited and out of breath that she wet her pants!

As was with everything in this country at that time, the train was segregated. Black people traveled in one car, while Whites in another. People on the train were very helpful with Burnie and me. She had to hold me on her lap most of the time because I was a very busy child. I didn't like to sit still. I wanted to venture around the train and observe the other passengers. I ping ponged through the train the entire trip. I was in awe of the blur of the fast passing forest and the crystal blue sky. Leaving Cincinnati, I saw tall buildings and concrete homes. I had only known wood shacks and vast countryside peppered with cotton fields. These city buildings were foreign to me and I was mesmerized. My entire world became new on that train.

My Mother was very tired when she completely settled on the train, but she was too excited to try to take a nap. She was busy looking out of the window seeing sights she had never seen. This was her first train ride. She was looking at the people on the train and listening to their conversations. This was a whole new world for her. Though we were only a few states from where we originated, the people on the train seemed to come from Mars. They spoke a different language and they acted as though they had seen all the extraordinary sights before. Not even books were able to show the wonders of my Mother's new world.

The long trip ended with a jolt. We exited the train, only to find my Father standing in wait. He looked handsome and like a Northern boy at the time. My Mother's mouth dropped when she saw my Father at the station gate. My Mother saw a new man, with a new way, who had transformed in just four months time. He was not the meek, mild, man who lived under his Father's thumb and left Alabama . He was a new man, in a new city, with a new life.

He took us to the house where we were going to be living and Mom was so excited that she could hardly contain herself. Daddy had rented two rooms on the third floor of this house and the bathroom and kitchen were on the second floor. Mom thought she had moved to Beverly Hills. Little did she know that one day, she would. This was her first experience with indoor plumbing and electricity. She said when everyone left the house, she would go downstairs and turn on the water and was amazed seeing it come from a faucet. She would constantly turn the lights on and off. She couldn't believe it.

Daddy had secured a job with the Pittsburgh Steel Mill and my Mother knew they would now have a steady income for the first time in their lives. When Daddy got off work, he would come home, have his dinner, shower, and take us for rides on the trolley to see Pittsburgh. This was an exciting time for us. My Mother said she had never seen so many lights, cars, restaurants, and buildings. It was exciting to see the trolley go up and down the steep hills of Pittsburgh. When the conductor stopped the trolley he would ring the large bell, beckoning joy and excitement from my sister and me.

It was very difficult for my Mother to get adjusted to the relationships between Black and White folks now that she was in the North. She had been conditioned in the South to dim her own light and kowtow to the whims of White people. The lessons that she learned were deeply ingrained and difficult to shake. They were written in stone on her heart and carved in her soul by years of oppression. Pennsylvania was totally different from Alabama. When my Mother would go to the store and encounter a White person and was asked a question, she would never look them in the face and always responded "yes ma'am or no sir." People would ask her where she was from and she would reply sheepishly, "Orion, Alabama." My Mother didn't raise her head when she spoke. Her deference was ever present. The notion that a Black person could answer a White person directly was completely foreign to her. Her experience of learning that her position as a Black woman meant not being able to be her full bold self was a lesson I took to heart and committed to change. I ultimately hypercorrected this by always looking people in the eye and never feeling as though I was invisible.

Pennsylvania was Shangri-la compared to Alabama. A year after our arrival, my parents rented a small apartment from a man named Mr. Davis. It had a living room, bedroom, kitchen, and bathroom. Burnie and I slept on a convertible couch. We lived in that apartment waiting for a larger place in a new federally financed housing project that was being constructed. The following year, my parents were notified that the two-bedroom project apartment was available. The apartment cost them $25.00 a month with all utilities included. Rent was based on your income. We now had a living room, dinette area, kitchen, two bedrooms, and one bath. We lived in the projects for four years, and Daddy's sisters, my aunts, moved from Alabama to live with us. They moved in with us along with my cousin Billy. This was their first time leaving the South. Billy became the little brother we never had. We enjoyed our time in the projects, because there were throngs of other children to play with. Everyone was friendly and it was like one big family.

Our play area was situated between two, four-story buildings. It was a fort of fun that we played in for hours on end. I particularly loved when it snowed. The banks of white fluffy flakes were the perfect canvas for spirited snowball fights and the construction of snowmen. I recall one blustery winter day I bounded outside to play. The moment I stepped from the stoop, I sank, feet first, into a sea of snow that swallowed me to my neck! My childhood was miraculous and beautiful, just like the first snow.

By 1945, my parents had saved enough money to buy our first home. It was a twelve-room house with three floors, plus a complete basement located at 6505 Shetland Street. The money for the down payment came from savings bonds that my Father earned from working. My Mother was an exceptional money manager and they agreed to use the bonds to buy the house. My parents rented out part of the second floor and the entire third floor. The rent helped them pay the mortgage. We lived on the first floor and of the other part of the second floor, as well as the basement with my Daddy's two sisters and one small child. My Father did all the repairs and was an amazing self-taught painter. He painted houses, churches, and storefronts as a side job to make extra money. He painted our Shetland Street house white, trimmed in blue. That color combination has followed each home that I have lived in ever since. It was the most beautiful house in the area. Mother put white curtains in each of the front windows and a black sofa and two oversized chairs with red cushions on the front porch. People would walk past our house admiring how beautiful it was. Nothing was that expensive, but Mother had excellent taste and she made it a home.

As a small child, I first realized that people can be jealous. They were jealous that I lived in a big beautiful house that was beautifully furnished. My Mother had an eye for design, so we always had a beautiful home. I never understood why people were jealous of our home though. I saw how hard my parents worked to have what we had. I always thought that folks wanted the rewards, but never the work. My dog was even subjected to the jealousy of others. He was a cute little Cocker Spaniel that frolicked in our backyard. I remember my Mother telling me to keep watch after him when he was outside because someone might throw poisonous food for him to eat in hopes that he would die. It was difficult. Even though we were all poor in a sense, other children would bully my sister and me because of our living circumstances. I don't think they hated us, we just had more than they did. They were blinded by the things, completely unaware of what my parents did to get us there. They would pick a fight with Burnie because she was very shy and timid. No one bothered me because I was tough and would fight anyone who stepped out of line or said a cross word about me or my sister. My grandfather, with all of his fight, lived in me. I loved Burnie and no one was going to take advantage of her. Some people thought I was mean but that wasn't true. I was never going to let anyone take advantage of me or my sister as young girls or adults. I have always stood up for myself.

When my Father's sisters moved out, my Mom started keeping foster children. These children came from homes where their parents were alcoholics, drug abusers, or faced child abuse. She opened our home to ensure that abandoned children would have care and love. She also knew that caring for children offered a steady income to create opportunity for them and our family. The Commonwealth of Pennsylvania had taken these children and placed them in foster homes because they often came from families that could not care for them. My Mother treated all of us the same. She knew the pain of being treated differently because of her own childhood with Georgia Mae. My parents never kept more than two foster children because my Mother wanted to make sure that all of us had equal time and attention, unlike what she experienced in her own childhood. She made sure that love was shared and spread with ease between all of us and that no one felt slighted.

To earn money and ensure that she could continue being a stay-at-home Mom, my Mother started baking sweet potato pies and selling them for 10 cents a slice. Burnie and I would gather our friends, so they could come and buy the pies. They were so delicious. She painstakingly peeled and smashed baked sweet potatoes. She added sugar, butter, milk, vanilla, and a menagerie of spices to create the perfect filling. Her pie crust recipe is still a secret, but it was buttery and flaky and the perfect vessel for the sweet, orange, silky, filling. When the word got out, people in the neighborhood would come and buy pies in droves. Two or three at a time, they would clamor for them. Mother would give Burnie and me a slice as payment after we sold the pies. We sold so many pies I think my fingers turned orange from the pie and green from the money that changed hands. Mommy was a fabulous cook. She started making Sunday dinners at our home and people from the neighborhood would come and eat dinner after church. Our home was open to everyone. My Mother had taken what she knew from that Troy, Alabama smokehouse and brought the spirit of community and sharing all the way to Shetland Street. Our house always smelled so good. My Mother was running an unlicensed restaurant in our home and no one minded. She had customers coming from everywhere. Thank God the authorities never found out.

My Mother started saving every penny she made from selling those pies. She learned from a real estate broker that if she could save $1,500.00, she could buy her first fixer-upper house. This was a family dream. She wanted it and she was determined to do it. One day she was at home alone cleaning and a voice came to her. As clear as day, it said "Eula, do it yourself, this is your dream." It was, indeed her dream. God, spoke to her and she wanted to carry the family with her. She purchased her first house in 1951 – 11 years after stepping off that train from Troy and arriving in Pittsburgh.

My Mother was smarter than her sixth-grade education suggested. She knew that property meant power, longevity, legacy, and wealth. She learned that lesson years before from her father-in-law as she watched him survey his 100 acres. The home that she purchased had three floors. In Pittsburgh, many families occupied the entire home. My Mother had other plans. In order to maximize the income, she rented out half of the second floor and the entire third floor.

Soon after that first purchase, she was able to own several houses totaling 33 rental units. She started a career owning and managing rental properties while my Father still worked at the steel mill. My Father was not pleased with her ambition, and it brought a lot of discord between them in the home. She was moving up and he was still at the mill. He paid the bills, but she paved the way. I think that he was intimidated by her success. My Mother never emasculated my Father, but I think that my Mother's determination and drive reminded him too much of his Father and he wanted nothing to do with that kind of success.

My Mother decided that she was not going to be poor all her life. She wanted more and she was determined to get it for herself and her family. She wasn't going to let anyone, including my Father, stop her. She wanted to be a stay-at-home Mom for me and Burnie and the other foster children that were in the house. She was adamant about being there for us if we needed her. She kept a watchful eye and an iron fist over her girls. My Mother was a dear Mother, but she didn't allow any antics that would shame the family name. She raised us to be independent, kind, respectful and responsible. My Mother demanded that we eat dinner as a family every night, no excuses. Those family dinners were the stage for spirited conversation and our parents reminiscing about their life in Alabama. They reminded us to always be kind, even in the face of jealousy or hatred. They stressed the importance of faith and family. They were affectionate, yet stern, and demanded academic and social excellence. When our friends joined us for dinner, they were treated as though they were family. In fact, our house was the house that everyone wanted to visit. My parents were loving and welcoming and there was never a shortage of hugs and kisses. They were also fiercely protective. I was only allowed to spend the night at a friend's house once. I don't think their protection was because they didn't trust my friends or their families, rather, they didn't see the need to spend the night in someone else's home.

Moving to The Lewis Estate

The Ira Lewis Estate was a beautiful piece of property in a private hilly area of Pittsburgh. The house was situated where beautiful stately homes sat with magnificent grounds that sprouted up like the plentiful cotton crops in Troy. The owner of the house was Mr. Ira Lewis. Mr. Lewis was the President and CEO of the *Pittsburgh Courier*. The *Courier* was the premier newspaper of Black society in Pittsburgh. By the 1930s, the *Courier* was one of the leading Black newspapers in the United States. Founded in 1907 by Edwin Nathaniel Harleston, the *Courier* was where the who's who of Black Pittsburgh shared their stories and accomplishments. He started the newspaper with his own money in an effort to showcase his poetry. In the late 1940s the newspaper was taken over by Robert L. Vann, another Black prominent writer and businessman.

The Lewis' sat at the top of the heap of Black bourgeoise in Pittsburgh. Their home was immaculate and the envy of all. After his death, Mrs. Lewis found it difficult to maintain the Estate and sought a buyer amongst the elite of Pittsburgh. My Mother, though not high society, had tenants on the third floor that were related to Mrs. Lewis. When she would visit, Mrs. Lewis always gawked at the furnishings in our home and shared her admiration with my Mother. At some point, Mrs. Lewis asked my Mother if she would be interested in buying the Estate. At this particular time in history, women didn't discuss things like property ownership and investments. Afterall, women were still given allowances from their husbands and couldn't obtain a credit card without a man's consent. Women were relegated to cooking, cleaning, and ensuring that their men had support. My Mother was different. She was a homemaker, but she was also a businesswoman with the foresight to see how she could build a legacy for her family and children.

My Mother was honored and excited that Mrs. Lewis asked her about purchasing the home. That night, my Mother asked Daddy about purchasing the Estate. He swiftly said "no" because he couldn't visualize living in such a large and stately home. Although my Father lived and worked in Pittsburgh, his mind was still living on the plantation in Orion. My Mother never took no for an answer. She told Mrs. Lewis that if she gave her time, she would find a way to purchase the coveted property. Over several months, my Mother continued to save her money and finally, in 1953, she told Mrs. Lewis that she had saved enough money to buy the home. What I marvel at, even to this day, is that Mrs. Lewis waited until my Mother had the money. She had several offers to buy the Lewis Estate, but she waited for my Mother to purchase her beloved home. Mrs. Lewis told my Mother that the Lewis Estate had to go to the right family, and ours was it.

We loved and enjoyed living in the Lewis Estate. The house was on four large lots with massive grounds, lush gardens, grand spruce trees, and fragrant rose gardens. It was a wood-framed house, with shingles on the roof, lined up in military order. Mom made changes immediately. Her first order of business was to enlarge four small front windows to large ones. This time, the white organza curtains in each window were custom made by a local seamstress. My Daddy painted the exterior and interior of the house. The outside was white, trimmed in blue and the inside featured forest green walls with snow white ceilings and baseboards. My Mother's eye for design shined brighter than ever in the Lewis Estate. She had the uncanny ability to take nothing and make it something magnificent. Her pride and joy were the pink plastic flamingos that were prominently placed on the lawn. I remember watching her position them in such a way, they looked like they were dancing in the wide green expanse of our front yard. It was a magical place to live.

The house was huge! The living room and master bedroom furniture were purchased at Gilbert's Fine Furniture, which was located on Smithfield Street in Downtown Pittsburgh. The furnishings were so beautiful that our home looked like it could be on the cover of *Architectural Digest* and it rivaled where we would ultimately live in Holmby Hills. It had a large living room, sunroom, dining room, piano room, breakfast room, and kitchen on the first floor with a bath. The second floor had four large bedrooms and two bathrooms. My parents also created a beautiful bar and party room in the basement. I remember hearing the clinking of glasses filled with punch and the dignified conversation between my parents and their friends. The scent of wax candles and fine perfume wafted through the vents and filled my bedroom. Their parties were legendary. Never to miss an opportunity to have a stream of income, my parents rented the garage in the rear of the house that had been transformed into a two-bedroom apartment. Life was good and we were a happy thriving family.

My bedroom was on the second floor. It housed a double bed, dresser, and a nightstand. My maternal grandmother had also moved in and her room was right across the hall from mine. I remember being able to hear her faint prayers and recitations of scripture in the night. She was a quiet woman who didn't cause a fuss. I loved her as a hallmate and having access to her and all of her wisdom. I would often sit on the floor in her room and listen to her tell stories about her upbringing. She talked about how she and my grandfather met and how she never had goals for herself other than to be a wife and mother. She told me about her time in Alabama and how hard her life had been living under the control of my grandfather. She taught me to stand up for myself and to never take abuse from anyone, especially a man. In many ways, I felt sorry for my grandmother. She was a sweet woman who had tremendous potential. Time and geography, however, didn't allow her to fully realize her possibilities. She is the very reason why I don't accept excuses from young people. They have the entire world in the palm of their hands and yet, far too many don't take advantage of the opportunities that are before them. It is a shame and it dishonors the ancestors.

When I think about it now, it's almost unbelievable. A timid share-cropper birthed a woman who would go on to become a successful real estate mogul. There is no way on God's green earth that that should be possible. These were women who had no examples of other women to model their lives after. How did she know that she could achieve? Afterall, my grandmother had no education and was hard pressed to speak at all. The idea that we all stand on the shoulders of men and women who, against all odds, did something extraordinary, blows my mind and makes me weep with gratitude. This woman, my hallmate and grandmother rested on a down-filled mattress with the softest sheets and most luxurious blankets. She would descend from her upstairs room in her silk bathrobe and find herself sitting in the breakfast nook sipping imported tea from a porcelain teacup. It's amazing how life can change with hard work and a little boldness. My Mother was able to do the impossible and we were all beneficiaries of her tenacity.

Learning the World of Real Estate

My Mother had acquired several properties and was always busy keeping an immaculate house, chatting with tenants, renting apartments, and making repairs. She was a full-fledged businesswoman in a time when women, not to mention Black women, were relegated to secretarial positions, teaching school, or cleaning homes. Career options for women were limited and predictable, but my Mother broke the code and chose a different way. This woman, who was fearful moving through the Cincinnati train station was now running a burgeoning real estate empire. Everyone in my family worked. I was tasked with collecting the rents from our tenants for her. I was driving at this time, so it was easy for me to do double duty as a teenager and rent collector. I would often pack my friends in my parent's 1951 black Buick or 1952 pink and white Cadillac to "help" me collect the rents. One of my dearest and closest friends, Fay Devereaux would often accompany me. She and I met in 1950 while attending Westinghouse Junior High School and we are still friends today. True friends were hard to keep in those days. She loved me because I was me, not because of what I had. Jealousy reigned when I was a teen and I would go to my Mother to seek wisdom from her to deal with the pains of the mean girls. My Mother was a practical woman who understood how it felt to be left out. She reminded me that what people think of me doesn't matter as much as what God thinks of me. I accepted her advice and never reciprocated the hatefulness that I experienced.

I recall one fateful day when Mother sent me to pick up some supplies in the Cadillac. She would always demand that Burnie and I exercise extreme caution when driving. She would often remind us of the dangers of driving and the potential of hurting ourselves or others. This day I had my rent collecting crew in tow and decided to crank up the radio. The stern admonishments of my parents drifted out of my head as the music drifted in. I have always loved music and I soon found myself lost in the bass and rhythm of the song. I don't recall what song pumped through the speakers, but it distracted me to such a degree that with every beat of the bass drum I lost more and more focus on my surroundings. In an instant, I hit the rear of a car in front of me. I had to pull over and get my identification out to show the driver. He was completely shocked to see a 17-year-old Black girl driving a new Cadillac. He was driving an older Chevrolet. He asked me whose car I was driving, and I told him that it belonged to my parents. He was perplexed that a family member would give such a young girl permission to drive such a beautiful car. Thank God I only bent his back fender. He did not claim that he was hurt but I knew that even though I sighed in relief at the accident scene, there would be another, more dangerous scene brewing at my parent's home when I got there in the dented Cadillac. Telling my Mother about the accident was awful. Even though the front bumper was the only bit of damage, telling her felt like I had totaled the car. As punishment, my Mother grounded me for two weeks. I learned my lesson and haven't had an accident since.

My Mother and Father believed in hard work, but they also required that we have fun. I think they pushed us to be footloose and fancy free because they were both prohibited from doing so in their teen years. After a long school week, I spent my weekends at school hops and dances at the YMCA on Centre Avenue or at parties at Knott Manor, which was an apartment house where we would host parties for our friends. We were all good kids with great ambition and promise. LeRoy Titus, James Henry, Diane Dean, Fay, and I were fast and faithful friends who spent our time partying together and planning our futures.

My leisure time gave way to business on the first of each month. Like clockwork, my Mother would beckon to me from the foyer all the way to my room, "Today the rents are due, La-Doris." Her voice was amplified a bit more on those days. There is something about a mother's voice. They have the uncanny ability to shake the walls and call everyone in the house to attention with one thundering statement. There was something about her tone that caused me to always take notice. She wasn't yelling, but her voice carried in such a way that I knew she meant business and every first of every month, I handled it.

Mother always required that we dress well outside the house. We were never permitted to wear slippers or clothes that were misshapen or dirty, not that we would have ever wanted to. We always had to be "pressed and dressed," as she often said. "Your last name is McClaney and we do things that are representative of that name, understood?" Not only did Burnie and I understand, but we carried that directive with us throughout our lives. Before attending to my duties, I would put on a simple dress and flat shoes so that I was appropriate and comfortable when it was time to collect the rent. My duties were conducted year-round and on the first of every single month, during winter, spring, summer, and fall, you could find me collecting rent and giving receipts for hours. I did that for years. In the wintertime, I would layer my clothes to provide my frame with a bit of insulation. No matter how harsh the weather, I could be found going door-to-door requesting the monthly rent from our tenants. On most occasions, I drove the black Buick, with my friends, packed six or seven deep to "help" me. We would position ourselves and stand at the tenant's door and when they opened it, they would be surprised to see so many of us. The older tenants had become accustomed to having a crowd of eager teenagers at the door. They would count out the money and I knew exactly how much they owed. When I recounted the money, I would give them a receipt that my Mother had made out. When they closed the door, my friends would gather around me and they would put the money inside a white handkerchief and pin the money inside my coat. I looked like a Christmas tree with money ornaments dangling from me. I learned early that tenants would come up with all types of excuses why they couldn't pay their rent. We would stand there and be very polite and listen. When the soliloquy was over, I would tell them, "my Mother told me to collect the rent, and I must return home with it, or else!" This experience gave me my first sense of dealing with people in a landlord-tenant situation. We would quietly laugh when a child came to the door and said, "my Mother told me to tell you she's not home." Nothing violent ever happened, but I did learn how to be firm when people became difficult. I felt bad for those that couldn't pay their rent, but I also felt bad for my Mother when they didn't pay. She had a mortgage and rarely did the tenants consider that my Mother was beholden to the bank. My Mother was so grateful for my skills, along with my friends because we were so successful in collecting rent every month.

After my duties were done, my Mother would give us money to go to The Original Hot Dog stand. We would pile into the shop and partake of the best hot dogs in Pittsburgh. We could hardly wait to taste the sweetness of the bun and the saltiness of the hot dog. On those days when we felt extra adventurous, we would venture across the street to the Italian sausage shop. They had the best hot Italian sausage sandwiches. Ooey gooey cheese danced on top of an all-beef sausage, nestled between the freshly baked Italian roll. Pittsburgh was a culturally diverse city and in turn, our cuisine was diverse as well. The mix of Italians and Quakers, Blacks, and the Polish, provided a variety of food offerings to tempt our palates. When all else failed, we could always go back to my house and snack on sweet potato pie from my Mother's kitchen.

Food was still a way to bring people together. Food was what drew the neighbors to the smokehouse. Food was how Georgia Mae contributed to the family. Food was what we sold to purchase the first property in Pittsburgh. Food was a celebration after a day of rent collection for a group of teenagers. Food was also how we celebrated in our family. My Father loved to take us to Bob's Big Boy for hamburgers. We considered it a huge treat to sit at a table and be served, often by White waitresses. My sister and I had sesame seed picking contests. Whoever picked all the seeds off the bun first was the winner. We didn't eat out often, but we did on occasion. My Mother was no longer cooking like she had on Shetland Street. She had graduated from a housewife to a businesswoman and in turn, her days were spent planning real estate purchases instead of planning meals.

My Father soon joined more actively in the business that my Mother established for our family. He was an expert painter and he taught me the art as well. After my rent collection duties were complete, I would often don overalls and a stained shirt and accompany my Father at the jobsites. He started me with small jobs painting radiators. I soon advanced to baseboards and doors. I could really handle a paintbrush. Painting was a side hustle that allowed my Father to earn money and contribute the necessary trade for the real estate business that my Mother had created. She saw it as a family business, even if my Father wanted little part of it.

Burnie was an exceptional seamstress. She sewed some of my clothes and the curtains for all the units that we owned. On top of our business duties, we were required to maintain our household chores. We washed dishes and dusted furniture. Burnie and I switched house duties weekly. I mowed the lawn with a push mower. We could afford a housekeeper and gardener, but my parents never considered having such extravagance.

High School Days

The greatest gift a parent can give their children is roots and wings. Roots are the ideals, standard, and beliefs that ground children and wings are the child testing out those roots in real-time in the world. Wings offer children the opportunity to become their full selves, while still maintaining their roots. For me, my first "flight" came in the form of driving. Driving was freedom for me. Even now, I love to drive. It is not unusual for me to hop in one of my several cars and drive four hours to Las Vegas or two hours to Palm Desert, for no particular reason at all. As a teen, I enjoyed driving around the city in my parents' black Buick. I would sit up in the driver's seat being really careful not to scratch or damage the car. Years later my parents would let Burnie and I drive to high school because at this time we had three cars in the family. Kids and teachers alike made no apologies for their hatred of seeing two Black girls driving these fine vehicles. It got to the point that I would sometimes park further away from school just so I didn't have to deal with the constant disparaging comments and looks aimed at me from the other students. I wasn't sensitive. I was just a high school girl with a healthy supply of self-doubt. I often wondered, "who *was* I to have such privilege?" My parents were born poor share-croppers in a small country town in rural Alabama that no one in Pittsburgh had ever heard of. My peers had no idea the strength and pure grit that ran through my veins. They had no clue that I was the descendant of people who decided, under impossible odds, to make a better life for me and my sister, and then did. I was the beneficiary of hard work, unimaginable suffering, and ultimately, hope. My parents had been raised by Jim Crow and rocked to sleep by systemic racism and the only thing these jealous teenagers and teachers could focus on was the kind of car that I drove. Now, looking back, I feel sorry for them. Because of their hatred of me they missed the blessing knowing their own possibilities by studying the example of my parents.

I never showed off or bragged about where my parents were living or that I rarely wanted for anything. I knew that our life wasn't always like that and I also saw the hard work that had to be done to keep what we had acquired. Everyone wanted the life but no one ever asked about the work that it took to have the life. I was called names, but never to my face. I never reacted with violence because I wanted to please my parents and be kind to everyone, even my enemies. I look back on pictures of my teen years and I see faces of people who would enjoy the spoils, only to later discover that they were talking about me behind my back while they danced and ate in my house. People are funny. Even then, they didn't wish me well and they didn't want **me** as a friend. They were only interested in what I had. It's a sad commentary, really. They missed the benefit of mutual care and admiration, and instead spent their time focusing on the material possessions that my parents had earned and being jealous of things that were temporal.

When we moved to the Lewis Estate, my parents let Burnie and I drive to high school because our house was approximately four miles from school. We could drive with one stipulation, that if we saw other students walking to school and there was room in the car, we were required to pick them up and take them to school too. If we didn't, the next day we would be walking that four miles, no matter what the weather looked like. Driving was a privilege and but for the grace of God, we would be walking too. She taught us early, even though we lived in a magnificent home with grounds of beautiful rose gardens and trees, we were never to think that we were any better than anyone else. It was the grace of God and their hard work that allowed us to live the way we did.

Westinghouse High School was an exciting place for me. Blacks made up about twenty percent of the student population, while Italians were about forty percent and Quakers were another forty percent. Burnie always had many more friends than I because she was more outgoing. It wasn't that I wasn't friendly, I could just read people and saw their insecurities and I had no interest in acquiescing to please people. I was social in my own way. I did not need a lot of friends, but I enjoyed having fun. I loved to sing and dance, even though my I was not a good singer. I can't hold a note in paper bag! I was, and still am, a fantastic dancer! I learned tap and ballet, and I had fabulous dancer legs. I noticed their beauty and so did the boys. They would make their feelings known, but my Mother was having none of it. In fact, dating wasn't even part of our life. We were a group of friends just wanting to have fun. Burnie was never interested in singing or dancing. She was a talented and gifted gossiper! I hated gossiping, and I still do. She was a girly girl and loved talking on the phone, about everybody. She was busy! I had no interest in sitting on the phone, talking about folks or recounting the events of the day that I had just experienced at school.

I found my passion when I discovered dance. A classmate of mine was taking professional dance classes at a studio. She would come back and teach a group of us the proper steps of the dances that she learned. I wanted desperately to be as skilled in the art as she was, so I practiced the steps day and night. Each time that she learned a new routine, she would beckon us to an empty corridor at school or onto the football field so that she could teach us what she had learned. We could not wait to put on our dancing shoes. Her name was Lois Dugan.

Lois was a tall, brown skinned girl with flowing jet back hair. Her walk was graceful and confident, and she had the best posture of anyone I have ever known. I used to think that she must have an additional vertebra in her neck because she was elongated from the top of her head to the soles of her feet. Her limbs were lithe, and she used them in a way that was beautiful and elegant. She was a dancer and I wanted to swallow all of her skill and grace to dance just like her. I would sit mesmerized while she taught the choreography that she had learned from her studio. I studied every move with a 1-2-3-4 and a 5-6-7-8 rhythm in my soul, dancing freely and with precision and passion. It was my first artistic love. And although I don't enlist the services of a choreographer, I can still cut a rug on demand when the beat hits me just right!

I became a confident dancer and wanted to share my talents with the student body. I was given a notice that the school talent show was upcoming. Much to Burnie's horror, I told her that I was going to enter the show. Being three years older than me meant that Burnie was a "cool kid" that could not be bothered with her kid sister performing at some talent show. I was unmoved by her disdain for my choice to show off my amazing talent. Arlene Jackson was a great pianist and played the violin. Her sister Edith was my piano teacher, but I never learned how to play because I didn't enjoy practicing the piano. Since playing the piano was out of the question, I decided to sing and dance instead, so I entered the talent contest and was permitted to perform. I practiced for a week to perfect my performance. Burnie complained to our parents that I was going to "ruin her reputation and shame the family name with my song and dance routine." Again, I was steadfast in my quest and unmoved. I would go over my dance steps in my head late into the night. I practiced every chance I got — in the house, in the backyard, in the basement, everywhere. When the day came for my grand performance, the auditorium was packed with students, parents, and faculty. Way in the back of the room was my horrified sister just waiting to melt into a small puddle when her kid sister brought the house down. I was backstage practicing my moves and I wasn't nervous at all. I had ice in my veins, and I was ready to perform like my life depended on it. I entered the stage with the confidence of a seasoned performer in a short, blue, and white dress and bright white patent leather shoes. When the music started, I was transformed into a Broadway dancer. I danced and sang my heart out. Chattanooga Shoeshine Boy was the song. I tapped and slid across the stage, twirling, and spinning in perfect rhythm. I finished my routine, out of breath having left everything I had on the stage. I bowed breathlessly and when I raised my head, I was met by an audience on their feet offering thunderous applause. Everyone enjoyed it. I was very pleased, but Burnie was totally embarrassed. I never understood why. She was three years older than me and about to graduate. I told her everyone loved it and it wasn't my problem she couldn't sing or dance. I laughed because deep down inside I knew she was jealous.

I was also an excellent swimmer and to graduate from high school, we had to swim the length of the swimming pool. I dipped my shapely form into the pool and made quick work of the required test. Tread water for 30 seconds. Swim the length of pool in less than a minute. Hold your breath underwater for 20 seconds. I completed my test and quickly jumped out of the pool toward the locker room. I wanted to make sure that the results of my wet hair didn't scare everyone off. Most of all I didn't want a particular boy to see what water did to my hair! I can't recall his name, but he was tall, dark, and handsome. I remember that he had a shy crooked smile that I adored. I did my level best to try to impress him, but my effort yielded me not even a look in my direction. I was completely invisible to him, and now, to me since I can't even remember his name. Boy, did he miss out!

Me and the rent collecting crew would often go to football games together. I loved going to the football games. I didn't understand the game then or now, but I enjoyed the excitement and comradery of fans rooting for our team. I also enjoyed going because there was a particular football player that caught my eye. After being ignored by the other nameless boy, I hitched my horse to another wagon and "fell in love" with this football player. In the winter it was freezing cold, as we sat on those cold benches laughing, giggling, and eating whatever we brought with us to the stadium. It was the interaction that I just loved. The group of us: Diane Dean, Anne Jones, LeRoy Titus, James Henry, and George Talley, had a steady standing at those games.

I would always be the driver to different parties because I had access to a car and loved dancing (as evidenced by my Chattanooga Shoe Shine Boy performance). I liked the boys and I was a party girl. I wasn't sexually active by any means, after all, my Mother's name was EULA McCLANEY and she was not one to play with. Frankly, I was always afraid of being sexually involved because I was constantly lectured that if I ever got pregnant before marriage, I could not live in their house. Secretly, I also think they would have literally killed me. They scared Burnie and me to death about being that type of busy. I did start smoking at a young age, along with Burnie. We would steal my Father's cigarettes and when our parents weren't around, we would sneak a smoke. That was the worst habit I could have ever picked up. None of my friend's smoked and they weren't pleased with me smoking, but I had the car, so they endured the vile habit. Thank God I had the sense of mind to quit when I did over thirty-five years ago. We never went to clubs because we were too young plus none of us ever drank liquor. I also had to have a sober mind to manage my parent's business.

Though, I never went to nightclubs, there was a club called The Crawford Grill owned by my friend's parents. I would go with her and her parents to listen to music and eat. The food there was so delicious. They had the biggest shrimp in the city and fried chicken that would make you cry with delight. Even though I was a picky eater, I enjoyed going to different restaurants. Burnie was the direct opposite. She would eat anything. She experimented with every cuisine on Earth. Her palette accepted any and everything. If it smelled bad, she ate it. If it looked bad, she ate it. Nothing was off limits. Burnie was an extrovert in every aspect of her life.

My parents were thrust into Black society because of the rapid and fervent growth of our real estate empire. They were always reluctant to run in those circles. Their lives had begun in a field and because of their status, now they trudged in ornate hotels instead of Alabama red clay and picked which invitation to accept instead of cotton. The once care worn leather shoes were replaced with fine clothing and heavily pressed dress shirts. They were unwilling members of the elite and they soon discovered that with this designation, certain rites of passage were necessary for them and for Burnie and me. None more important than the Debutante season.

Members of the Links, Incorporated Pittsburgh Chapter approached my Mother to invite Burnie to participate in their annual Debutante Ball. These balls were designed to celebrate its young female participants and introduce them to society. It is an ancient practice that has stood the test of time and is still practiced today. Young women don white gowns and are presented to the ball guests. A narrative of her accomplishments is recited as she's paraded across a large dance floor by her Father. This pomp and circumstance was exactly the type of attention Burnie craved. The Ball also requires that the Debutante dance with her Father and, later, her escort. My Father didn't dance. In fact, he didn't know how to dance. There wasn't much time for such things in his youth or his adulthood, for that matter. When Burnie was presented, a stand in was used. My Father humbly obliged because he didn't want to embarrass himself or Burnie. She was stunning that night. I watched as she glided effortlessly across the dance floor with the stand in. I remember my parents beaming with pride as the Master of Ceremonies read her accomplishments. My admiration was interrupted when my mind shifted to a much more practical question, "I wonder how much all of this cost?" I leaned over to my Mother and asked. I was met with a stern look and a pursed lipped response, "Not now La-Doris. We will discuss this later." I leaned back into my seat and returned my gaze to the sea of white gowns waltzing in perfect unison. This rite of passage for the girls in our social circle seemed a bit over the top in my book. It was self-celebratory and I didn't want to have any part of that. I knew that my Mother wanted it for me, but I didn't want it for myself. Knowing my feelings, when we arrived home my parents sat me down and offered me the choice, "La-Doris, when it's time for you to make your debut, would you like to participate in the Ball or would you like the amount of money that we spent on Burnie's Ball?" I asked how much money they had spent, and they told me $1500.00. I promptly asked for a check and made my way to my room knowing that I would never have to don a white gown, waltz across a dance floor, nor have my accomplishments read aloud to the members of Black society in Pittsburgh and I was perfectly fine with that. The irony is that today, I have been a member of the Links, Incorporated for over 36 years.

I was proud of myself that day. It was the first real time that I was allowed to negotiate and broker a deal with my parents. In those days, parents were the last word, period. My parents, though strict, were progressive too. My Mother would invite our opinions and ideas into the conversation. She had spent her life watching as her mother was silenced and I know that she wanted something different for us. I think that she did so because she wanted to make sure that we knew that we had a voice and that our voice mattered, even if it was in direct conflict with what she wanted. She would always listen, offer another perspective, and then do what she wanted to do anyway!

Being in business has made me become more of an extrovert. I didn't start off that way. In fact, I had to learn how to be social. Burnie loved everyone and was known as "Miss Personality." I never understood how she could like everybody. She had hundreds of friends and I didn't. My circle was and remains very small. I know a lot of people, but I have very few friends. Burnie was often taken advantage of because of her generous heart. At times I think that her friendships were based on what she could give to her friends, rather than just true admiration and love. I never wanted relationships like that. I had experienced that kind of hurt early in my high school years and I vowed never to experience that again.

While I was a sophomore in high school Burnie, who had graduated 3 years before me, decided to attend Morgan State University in Baltimore, Maryland. I was devastated at the idea of her leaving me. I imagine that my Mother felt the same way when Georgia Mae ran off and eloped. Burnie leaving for college felt like a loss of which I didn't think I would ever recover. Her leaving was painful. For so long it was just she and I being teenagers and having fun. Now, with her leaving I wondered who would stick up for her. Who was I going to rely on to tell me what dress looked good on me and which one didn't? Burnie was my best friend and she was moving on in her life and leaving me in Pittsburgh.

When it was time for Burnie to leave for college, my heart broke. We sneaked a cigarette and reminisced about our time together at the Lewis Estate. My Mother never liked the fact that Burnie and I smoked. She never saw us smoking but she could smell the smoke on us and she was disgusted by the habit. I can imagine that had my Mother caught us smoking, this book would not be in your hands because she would have killed me and Burnie! Burnie was on her way to Baltimore, Maryland to attend Morgan State University and I was going to be alone at home. A hole was in my heart when Burnie left. She was happy that she was going away to start a new and exciting life in college and getting away from her singing, dancing little sister. She was grown and it was time for her to be amongst people her own age. She left Pittsburgh gleeful and hopeful for the future. I wept watching her pack.

Right before her send off, we decided to have a huge summer bash at the house. We hosted the first and only Bermuda Shorts Party at the Lewis Estate. It was the party of the year. The attire was Bermuda shorts. Everyone in town wanted to attend. When the rumors of our party began to stir in the neighborhood, even those that were not so fond of us started being friendly because they wanted to get the coveted invitation. This was the one time that my Mother allowed us to shun those who had been so hateful. We didn't invite them. Burnie said, "let them hear about our party on the radio and see what they are missing." I said, "Amen!" Our guests made sure to attend in their finest outfit because everyone who was anyone would be there to party with us. My Mother asked Mr. Coleman, our neighbor and family friend, to come to the house a couple of days prior to the party to prepare all the meat. Chicken, ribs, ham, you name it – all barbecued to perfection on an open grill. My Mother and her friends prepared all the other side dishes. A disc jockey named Bill Powell brought his DJ equipment from the studio to the house and set it up to do his radio show. The party was broadcast live on WAMO radio, the Black radio station of the day, which still broadcasts on 107.3.

There were at least 250 teens in our backyard. We danced and ate and laughed into the wee hours of the night. We had a ball! I was able to showcase my dancing skills by doing the Twist. We twisted all day and night. By the time we awakened the next morning, there was no grass to be found in the yard. We had twisted it into oblivion. Mother didn't care. She was determined to give her girls the life that she dreamed of when she was picking cotton in Troy. A life of joy and fun, favor, and access. She gave us that and so much more. What God had in store for us was well beyond her dreams and even though we had gotten to a comfortable place in life, it was all just beginning.

Going to Los Angeles

In 1957 my Mother wanted to get away from Pittsburgh and take a vacation. She had spent most of her time purchasing properties, fixing them up, and renting them out. She rarely had time to just rest and relax. She was exhausted. It was a full-time job that she did at home, all while raising two daughters and supporting my Father as a dutiful wife did in those days. My Father was still working at the Pittsburgh Steel Mill and painting properties on the side. They worked tirelessly for many years and made no time for themselves, let alone a family vacation. My Mother's decision to go on vacation was a welcomed departure from the usual hustle and bustle of life that we had grown accustomed to. My parents decided that California was the perfect vacation spot for our family. Sun, surf, and sand drew us to the West Coast that summer. We were all excited to go and spend time as a family like we had done on those trolley rides around Pittsburgh so many years before. As we were packing to leave, my Father decided not to join his family on the trip. I don't know why he made such an abrupt decision days before our scheduled departure, but he did. Looking back, I think I knew that decision would ring in the ears of our lives forever, but I didn't know how loud it would ultimately become. I was heartbroken because I wanted him to travel with us. I was so looking forward to the four of us just being together, without work or duties to complete.

Me and my Dad had always had a special relationship. He taught me how to paint and I would listen to him talk about his life and the harshness of his Father and the vacantness in his heart having lost his

53

Mother. I never minded his pursuit for painting perfection because I knew that, in a way, painting was therapeutic for him. He loved me and shared his life with me over buckets of paint while wearing overalls. We grew closer with every splatter and as we cut the edges between ceiling and walls. Painting was a metaphor for our lives. Strokes of color colored walls as conversation and laughter colored our time together. I missed him. I wanted him with us – with me, with his family.

The day that we left, we packed up the car and bid my Father farewell. Driving across country with my Mother, my sister, my cousin Billy, and my grandfather in tow. The trip was long and wonderful. I remember looking out of the window taking in the beauty of the country. I was the same observant child that traversed the train on our trip from Troy to Pittsburgh. I watched as the trees turned from the white oaks of Pennsylvania to the bald cypresses of Oklahoma, the Arizona desert-willow, to finally the stately palm trees of California.

We stopped to soak up the diversity of the states. We were in no hurry to get anywhere, so we had plenty of time to absorb it all. We had a blast on that trip. As always, my Mother had prepared food for the road. You haven't lived until you've eaten a slice of sweet potato pie sitting on a bench at a New Mexico rest stop surrounded by everyone you love. It gets no better! We snacked on fried chicken and potato salad and washed it all down with an ice-cold pop. We arrived in Texas on our third day of travel and our fourth and our fifth! Texas was massive. We thought that we would never step foot on the California sand.

When we laid eyes on those palm trees, it felt like we had entered a whole new world. California was nothing like Pittsburgh. Pittsburgh was a wonderful place to grow up, but since its founding in 1758, not much had changed. It was an old city. The buildings were predictably brick and grey with the soot from the residue of the steel mills. The sidewalks were cracked, and the overgrown tree roots caused them to buckle and break. Don't get me wrong, I love Pittsburgh because it was my home, but crossing the state line into California was like entering a whole new world. When we saw that first row of palm trees we started hollering and screaming to the top of our lungs. There they stood in orderly lines overlooking the expanse of stucco buildings and shiny cars, green grass, and smooth grey sidewalks. We were finally in California.

My Mother had been to California earlier at a Baptist convention and had always talked about her California experience with great admiration. I recall after she returned from that trip that Burnie and I sat at her feet listening to her talk about this magical place . When we arrived, we stayed with a family friend for a week until we found a motel on Western Avenue. The motel that we selected happened to be owned by a Black woman. We had never experienced motels in Pittsburgh, and certainly not one owned by a Black woman. We checked in and got settled. During our stay, my Mother, ever the inquisitive person that she was, befriended the owner. True to form, my Mother became increasingly curious about how to operate a motel and how she would be able to purchase it. There was something special about the motel business that intrigued my Mother and she didn't let the owner rest until she learned everything about the business. By the time I looked up, my Mother had secured a real estate broker and we began looking at motels for sale all over the city of Los Angeles. We visited all the sites in Los Angeles, Beverly Hills, and Hollywood. It felt like we looked at 100 motels before we found Flagstone Motel. Once she set her sights on Flagstone, my Mother was laser focused on buying it. It always amazed me that she was so driven that even on vacation, she was building our business. Some people may have been bothered by her focusing on business during a family vacation, but we weren't because she was continuing to plant the seeds of the legacy for family. We understood her motivation and appreciated her commitment to the family.

The day she called my Dad to tell him about Flagstone she was met with a welcomed enthusiasm about the purchase. She told him that the motel would be a great place for the family to vacation to during those cold blustery Pittsburgh winters. He agreed and cheered her on with the purchase. My Dad knew how my Mother was. She made no apologies for wanting more for us and she wanted the family involved with every decision. She honored my Father in every way and consulted him on all the decisions that she wanted to make. His only question was related to the down payment and where the funds would come from to make it. My Mother never hid anything from my Dad, and she was always upfront about our financial position. She had purchased stocks earlier and they had matured enough where she was able to cash them out and pay the down payment for Flagstone with no problem. He didn't fully understand the "how," but he knew her and that was enough for him to bless the purchase. They were a rare couple in 1957. She asked him to accompany the family in California, partly because she missed him, and partly because she wanted to share the experience with him and Burnie and me. He agreed to come to California in the winter months. I was elated. Afterall, I am a Daddy's girl through and through.

Flagstone Motel was located on Washington Boulevard, west of La Brea Avenue. At that time, Black people had not ventured that far west. That area was designated for the White middle-class. The only Black faces that were seen in that area in those days, were those boarding buses after a day working in the homes of White folks. My Mother changed that narrative forever the day she set her sights on Flagstone. We were the first to crack that glass ceiling. After the paperwork was completed, the broker presented it to the owners of the motel. They refused to sell it to us because she was Black. California was the most liberal state in the Nation at the time, but even then, your skin color could prevent you from buying a property that you were more than qualified to purchase. They masked their blatant bias by saying that they didn't want to sell to an out-of-state buyer, but that wasn't true. They didn't want an uppity Black woman buying property in that area. My Mother never accepted "no" for an answer. She was provided for like Abraham and given a ram in the bush.

My Mother called a friend of hers named Betty Lewis who was a Black woman with very fair skin. Betty could pass for White on any given day and she used that to her advantage. At the time, many light-skinned Black people would "pass." Historically, passing afforded Black people the ability to escape the virulent oppression that led to their enslavement, segregation, and brutalization. Being able to pass for White sometimes meant the difference between a life in captivity and a life of freedom, and in this instance, it meant the ability to buy a piece of property in a desirable part of town. Mrs. Lewis was not shy about using her skin to get what she wanted, and she extended the courtesy to my deep-toned Mother. Mrs. Lewis believed in my Mother's mission to own real estate. She championed my Mother's efforts as often as she could. She was the person that encouraged my Mother to venture to California to explore a new market for real estate outside of Pittsburgh. My Mother knew that Flagstone was going to be a part of her real estate portfolio. She also knew that her black skin prevented her from growing her business in the way that she desired. She figured that if White skin would allow her to build her legacy, then she would ask her friend to act as a straw man in this purchase. My Mother asked Betty Lewis to purchase the motel for her and when it closed, she could quit claim it back to my Mother. Betty agreed to make the deal without hesitation and when she approached the owners, they told her a woman from Pennsylvania wanted to purchase the motel, but they didn't feel comfortable because she "wasn't from California." The racism in real estate was, and still is bold and brazen. Black people were only supposed to buy property in the Black community or the "ghetto" as those areas have been coined. Nowadays, they use terms like "urban," "densely populated," or "the heart of the city." We all know those are code words for predominantly Black areas. The real estate industry wanted to relegate Black people to specific areas where we could own property. We were to stay in our place and out of their way. My Mother had other ideas. We maintained our properties in both areas in the same way. We also did not allow anyone to dictate where we could buy, even if that meant using a straw man (or in this case, a straw woman) to complete the sale. It's the covert racism that is the worst kind. We knew that they didn't want us there and that is exactly why we **HAD** to be there. That fearless effort opened the door to so much more and we were glad to crack the ceiling and provide a ladder for others to climb up.

PHOTOS

La-Doris McClaney

Me & Burnie

Joanna Holt Hendrick

Joe Frank Hendrick

Me in High School

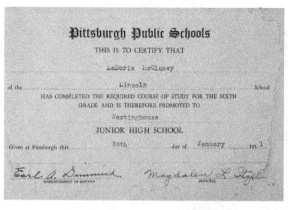

Junior High School Diploma

Me in Elementary School   Burnie

My parent's home

Me and my father

My Beloved Mother

Burnie and I

Tommy Lee & Jimmie Lee

At McClaney Estate – Holmby Hills

My Mother, Mrs. Rosa Parks, and Me

Launching my Mother's book, *God, I Listened*

My beloved foster children

Dorothy Ellis, R.N

Me

Me receiving my Ph.D. at
Bethune Cookman University

Me and Dr. Terri Gibson

With the Board of Trustees of Bethune-Cookman University

Oxford Building

UCLA Building

Cloverdale Building

Dr. La-Doris McClaney School of Performing Arts and Communication
Bethune-Cookman University

My Rolls Royce

Me and Ledley Smith in China

Flagstone Motel

Betty Lewis

Me and Samuel L. &
LaTanya Jackson

Burnie, Nate Hall, Me,
President Gerald Ford and my Mother

Tommy, Me, Cookie,
& Magic Johnson

Glynn Thurman, Me,
& Richard Lawson

Me & Lou Gossett, Jr.   Ondra Lewis & Mayor Tom Bradley

Celebrity impersonators *Marilyn Monroe, Michael Jackson*, Me & Tommy

Me & Tommy & Jacki

Pastor Frank Wilson

Me & Tommy

Dr. LeRoy Vaughn

With Linda Hopkins

Iris Dance Murray
My Mentor

McClaney's Holmby Hills Estates

Ballroom at McClaney Estate Holmby Hills

Me and Tommy

Me and Tommy at Mayor Tom Bradley's home

Fay Devereaux

Mommy's Mercedes Benz

Pastor Chuck Singleton, Marilyn McCoo, and Billie Davis, Jr.
at the Gospel Songfest

Me, Tommy, and Nancy Wilson at the Crystal Ball

McClaney Estate - Las Vegas

Me in my Abaya in Dubai during my visit with the Royal Family

Me and Dorothy Ellis at Juma's Camel Farm

Ebrahim Shaaban Abdullah and Juma Mohemmed Sultan Al Khaili

Los Angeles declared January 16, 2015 as Dr. La-Doris McClaney Day

By Sentinel News Service
Published January 31, 2015

On behalf of 3.8 million Angelenos,
L.A. City Council honors African American woman who gave millions

Janice Smallwood-Mackenzie, Lady Mae L. Blake, & Jacki Castillo

Zelma Willette, Norma Archie, and
Esther Alexander
"The Golden Girls"

Ikie Heard

Denise Turner,
my favorite cousin

Pastor Clinton and
Dr. Mary House

Me & Tommy

Bishop Charles E. Blake, Sr, Lady Mae L. Blake, Me, & Tommy

PART III

Los Angeles, California

New Beginnings

We knew what the motel owner's problem was — we were Black. My Mother had perfect credit and had the money to buy Flagstone, but she was still unable to complete the purchase without the help of Betty Lewis and her white skin. Her black skin trumped her green dollars. As always, she was able to circumvent the oppression and she created a way out of no way. She listened. My Mother always had the ability to do that. She could see a problem that, for most, would seem insurmountable, and she found a way to make her desires a reality. She was bold enough to believe that she could do anything she set her mind to. I learned that from her. I rarely take "no" for an answer. There is ALWAYS a ram in the bush! When God places a goal or desire in my spirit, I know that He will also make a way to manifest it in my life. God is creative in how He operates, and I love that about Him. He has the amazing ability to give you the desires of your heart, protect you from things YOU think you want, and enrich and strengthen His power in your life, all at the same time. I open my heart and mind and He, in return, floods my life with blessings and the most amazing testimonies. I am not special. I am merely a woman who has decided to walk, listen, and heed the Word of God. I had the best possible example of how to do that in my Mother.

While we were in California, my Mother requested that Burnie come home from college because she knew that Burnie was able to handle the financial records and other administrative duties. Burnie was stepping in, and I was moving on. I went away to Tennessee State University (TSU) in Nashville after the first trip to California and the purchase of Flagstone in 1958. My Mother wanted me to experience life in the South, even if for a year, in order to better understand my roots. Going away to school was an exciting time, but I knew that it is was going to be a short-lived adventure. God can often delay plans in order to use you more effectively in the season that you are in. When my college career ended at TSU, I went back home and rejoined my family in California. Running Flagstone Motel was an extraordinary time of life for us. Although we were the only Blacks at that time living west of La Brea on Washington Blvd., we enjoyed our time there. We became fast friends with our next-door business neighbors, the Frances Drive-In. We would walk next door to get food. The drive-in was a frequent stop for the White middle-class residents that lived nearby. The Frances Drive-in had a chef named Willie Redd. At the end of the night, he would often bring his nightly cuisine to us for dinner. Willie Redd made the best food that I had ever eaten.

When clients came to rent a room and saw us, they would ask about the Jones family — the former owners. They saw our Black skin and you could see the fear in their eyes. We would tell them that we were workers and the Jones' were on a long vacation. They always paid and we would laugh as we placed their payment in the cash drawer. Their green money trumped their White skin.

Daddy decided not to join us in California as he said he would. He broke his promise and my heart. I don't know to this day why he changed his mind, but it was a turning point for our family forever. At the time, I did not understand why he said one thing and did another. When my Mother left Pittsburgh, my parents were on good terms. I think that he was too proud to admit that he didn't have the same ambition as my Mother. Her dream wasn't his. As much as they loved each other, my Father didn't want what she wanted, even if it would benefit them both. She reminded my Dad of his own father and he resented her success. He wanted a simple life and my Mother wanted a legacy. She understood that he was his father's son and needed to be that man for himself. Thinking about it now still breaks my heart. Not because I wanted them to force the will of one on the other, but because they could have talked it out and perhaps compromised. I just wanted my family together again.

My Father ultimately came to Los Angeles for a brief visit and seemed to enjoy it. True to form, he painted the office at Flagstone a beautiful shade of blue. As always, I assisted him. When he was done, he returned home, and unceremoniously filed for divorce from my Mother. I remember the day that she found out that he no longer wanted to be married to her. I sorted the mail that came to the motel every day. Rarely, if ever, did we receive a certified letter, but this day, we did. The return address showed *616 Wilkinsburg Avenue, Pittsburgh, Pennsylvania*. The Lewis Estate. I bounded into my Mother's office and plopped the letter on to her desk. She examined it and then opened it. A stillness fell on her face and her eyes welled up with tears. I had never seen my Mother's heart break until that day. "Your Father has asked for a divorce. He doesn't want to be married to me anymore," she said with a shake in her voice. Gone was the thunderous sound that I was used to hearing leave her mouth. This time, she sounded frail and sad. It was a sound that I had never heard from her. My Mother was not a cussing woman, but I think she may have said a few zingers that day. She spoke those words and then she sat quiet and motionless for a moment. She then picked up the phone. I excused myself because even though I was grown, I didn't want to know anything about this situation. I wanted no part in the sorted details of their marital demise. Walking out of that office I felt my heart break at the hands of my Father again. That cold feeling that runs through your body at a sight or sound of something dreadful is what I experienced. How could he? It was a cold way to convey a life-changing message. It was cruel and heartless. When my Mother emerged from the office, her tears were gone, and she began handing out instructions to me. Dutifully, I sat and listened and jotted down every word she spoke. She had turned off her emotions and got down to business.

Under no circumstance would I have ever expected my Father to ever file for divorce. They had their conflicts, but I didn't see a divorce coming at all. They were good people who just looked at life differently. When I look back over my life, I think it was the best thing for the two of them. It allowed them to be free to be their authentic selves, but at the time that it was happening, I didn't understand why he chose divorce. My Mother always said she would never leave my Father. Everything she ever accomplished was for her family. My Father was the love of her entire life. She loved him from the moment they began exchanging love letters in Troy. She loved him as they worked in the fields in the hot Alabama sun. She loved him when she saw him after that first train trip to their new life. She loved him while he painted the office at Flagstone, and she loved him even after that certified letter altered the sequence of her life, forever. Theirs was a pure, but complicated kind of love and now, their marriage was over. Because she couldn't face the sadness and grief of her lost marriage and the memories from that house, she sent me to retrieve all her things from our beloved Lewis Estate.

My role has always been to conduct the business of our lives. Burnie built relationships, my Mother articulated ideas, and I executed the work. I have always been the doer. My job was to do the work of the business, whether it was real estate or in a family crisis. I was charged to handle it all. I arrived in Pittsburgh to complete the task given to me by my Mother. My mission was singular - retrieve the furniture and trinkets that she treasured and ship them home to California. I have the amazing ability to compartmentalize things and can separate feelings and emotions from business dealings. My task was not to be done as a daughter whose parents divorced, but as a woman charged with doing what was asked of me. My Mother contacted

Allied Van Lines and made all the arrangements for moving. It cost $3,000 to move her furniture to California. The van pulled in front of the Lewis Estate while I sat on a chair reminiscing about the Bermuda Shorts party and how beautifully the grass had grown back. I thought about the first night we spent there and the forest green walls and elaborate velvet curtains. I fell into a sadness because I knew that I would never live in the Lewis Estate again with my family intact. That dream died and left and, in its wake, was a new reality fraught with unknowns and uncertainty. I didn't have time to think about it any longer though, the furniture was waiting for me just beyond the double doors. Daddy allowed me to take all of the furniture she had purchased. When I looked into my Father's face as I entered the house, he was sad and withdrawn. The house that was once bustling with excitement and parties, was quiet and cold. He was alone when I arrived, and we stood face-to-face unsure of what to say to each other. In awkward fashion, we made pleasantries and talked about the weather as the movers began taking the pieces of my family from our home and placing them in the back of a truck. It was if we were dissecting our life and storing the memories in neat, shrink-wrapped packages. I couldn't bring myself to ask him why he decided to divorce my Mother, and to seek it in such a brutal manner — by certified mail. It was cruel to get a letter that ostensibly said, "this relationship is not even worth a phone call." I never asked why, I just loved them through it. It was devastating. I was grown and it was still devastating.

When the movers were done, I decided to leave Pittsburgh. The flight home was awful. There I sat, by myself reflecting on what had happened. Not just what happened earlier in the day, but what happened in the days, weeks, months, and years prior. Where had it gone wrong? When did he know he wanted to leave her? Did he ever love her? Did he really love me? I watched the clouds that hung gently in the sky from the airplane window. I saw my family life dissipate like mist and float away. I wept. Divorce, when there are children involved, is awful. Burnie and I were the receptacles of all the hurt that the divorce caused. I wasn't privy to the interworking's of their relationship, but I was selfish in the sense that I just wanted my family together like the old days. It was difficult for me to say goodbye to my Daddy. I wasn't sure what the divorce would do to my relationship with my Father, but I knew it would be different. It was. I resented him for years, not because of the divorce, but because of how he presented it to my Mother. The divorce took a toll on me and Burnie. We were all blindsided and that was unfair. My Mother had always been fair to him, but in this instance, he hadn't been fair to her. She didn't talk about the divorce, ever and she never spoke an ill-word about my Father. She didn't understand why he wanted out of their marriage, but she respected his wishes. She was hurt and angry. Upon my return from Pittsburgh, she watched as the furniture was being unloaded and she wept. My Mother gave my Father everything except a for some units that she continued to own in Pittsburgh when they divorced. All she asked for was the furniture and trinkets that sat prominently on shelves and bookcases in the house. I was furious with her for giving it all away to the man that broke her heart by certified letter. All I could think about was the thousands of sweet potato pies and long hours building an empire, those cold winter days collecting rents and those hot and humid summer days cleaning and painting apartments, preparing them for a new tenant. She gave it all away without any reservation or a second thought. Seeing my frustration, she explained to me that nothing that she obtained was worth damaging relationships with people that she cared about. I thought, "what relationship? It's over! The damage was already done." She said, "La-Doris, never burn bridges. You never know if you must cross it again. That man is your Father and he and I loved each other deeply at one time. You **WILL** honor and respect him or you will answer to me." I heard her loud and clear. I was to be my Father's daughter and not be the in the middle of or have an opinion about my parents' relationship. Their marriage was over and so was the fantasy that I created for myself about our family and their relationship. Life is funny that way. It will always sneak up on you and give you a healthy dose of reality. My Mother had created our new family reality despite the callousness of my Father. Our family legacy was solid and growing by leaps and bounds. She decided that divorce was not going to break her. She wasn't going to let stuff or money ruin what my parents had and tarnish the memories that they shared. No one could erase the past, and if she was able to amass that wealth once, then she would be able to do it again. And we did.

The motel ran smoothly. My Mother, Burnie, Georgia Mae, and I made sure the rooms were clean and in accordance with our chore schedule. Even though we still owned a handful of units in Pittsburgh, we all worked other jobs. After four months at the motel, Georgia Mae returned to Detroit to be with her family. Burnie secured a job at Crocker Bank as a teller, and I got a job at the Los Angeles County Sheriff's Department as a teletype operator. I worked at the Sheriff's Department for six and a half years, all while moonlighting at the motel. In the divorce, my Father took most of our real estate holdings, including the Lewis Estate. She was determined to resurrect her real estate empire in California, while my Father lived comfortably in Pittsburgh at the Lewis Estate.

The Sheriff's office was my first *real* job, and I was able to discover what it was like to work somewhere other than with my family. I enjoyed my time there, as it taught me that managing people is an art and a science. As a supervisor, you set the tone for your staff. I took many of the lessons from my experiences as a teletype operator into our family business, and I still utilize them today. When I felt like I wasn't treated correctly at my job, I was courageous and empowered to use my voice. That type of bravado from a Black woman wasn't always appreciated in the 1960s, but I learned that I mattered that day in Pittsburgh when my Mother discovered that she could look people in the eye. Because of that experience, I never cast my eyes down and I never allow my voice to be silenced.

I left the Sheriff's Department in 1965 to get married and move to Europe. The marriage ended in annulment and I spent four months traveling all over Europe. It was a wonderful time in my life. When I returned to the United States, I stopped off in New York City for two months and worked for Chase Manhattan Bank as a teletype operator but quickly realized that I was needed at home to help with the family business.

Murder at the Flagstone Motel

In 1965, Burnie and I, along with now Congresswoman Maxine Waters, went to San Francisco for a freedom march to protest the murder of Reverend James J. Reeb. Reverend Reeb was a White universalist minister who heeded the call on Bloody Sunday and marched alongside Dr. Martin Luther King, Jr., as they traversed the Edmund Pettus Bridge in Selma, Alabama. We had always fought for Civil Rights and this march provided an opportunity for us to make our voices heard. When we arrived in San Francisco we were met by a sea of people all expressing their desire for the equal treatment of Black people. We left that weekend inspired and determined to change the landscape of Black life in America. We believed in the power of the human spirit and the good that the world had to offer.

When we arrived home, we were on a high. Life seemed to be calming and the business was booming. My Mother was very proud of herself because she had run the motel smoothly without Burnie and me. When we got to Flagstone, my Mother was a little concerned because she said there was an unusual smell coming from one of the rooms. She hadn't made much of it, but her face told a different story. She was worried about it and I think that she was too afraid to address it to any large degree. At the time, my cousin Marion Baker and her son, Gordon "Twig" Baker, had moved in with us. Twig loved my Mother and would always stay very close to her when his Mother was at work. Twig and my Mother were very similar, they were both inquisitive and funny. There's was a love that was reminiscent of my Mother with her father-in-law — they just understood each other.

Twig, as his nickname suggested, was a small, slight boy. He had big beautiful brown eyes and soft features. His smile was sly, and his brown skin glowed like gold. He was the only boy that was around and even with his small stature, he carried himself like he was the man of the house. When he wasn't conducting his manly duties like taking out the trash or tending to small maintenance jobs, he could be found playing around the motel grounds. Twig was known as the unofficial mascot of Flagstone. He knew everything that happened on the property and could identify every patron, their room number, and could tell you everything they did or said.

According to my Mother, the unusual smell was emanating from room #2. Because Twig knew everything about everyone who stayed at the motel, he was the first to open the door of room #2. He was, after all, the man of Flagstone and he took his role very seriously. He confidently said, "Don't worry…I'll check it out." As soon as he opened the door, his already large brown eyes grew to saucer size. The smell hit us like a ton of bricks and almost knocked us out of the room. Undeterred and focused, Twig ventured further into the room and eventually made it past the bed to the coat closet. There, he found the body of a woman. He originally believed the body to be a doll, but the decomposition confirmed our greatest fear. He ran out of the room as fast as lightning. He was panting and his golden skin had transformed to an ashen grey hue. His sly smile was down turned, and he was hot with fear. Twig's discovery was scary. I thought my Mother was going to have a heart attack right then and there. All the color drained from her face and she was stiff with fear.

My Mother immediately called her attorney James E. Morgan, a prominent Black attorney with a practice in Los Angeles. He had been admitted to the California Bar in 1957. Mr. Morgan had previously advised us on several legal matters and was a trusted advisor and friend. It may have seemed strange to call an attorney after finding a body in the closet of a room at the motel that you owned, but as a Black woman who owned a motel in that area where we weren't readily welcomed, an attorney was on speed dial. James instructed us to call the police department to tell them about the body we had found in the closet. They assured us that they would send help. As the police arrived, James did too. He brought along a friend of his who had a close relationship with the police department. Along with my Mother, he was able to explain how the discovery was made. I was shaken because I had never experienced anything like that in my life. James hadn't either. After his conversation with the police, he walked across the street to the Liquorama and swiftly took 3 shots of liquor to calm his nerves. The police asked so many questions and they did so for hours. My Mother showed the police the registration card the people signed and answered all their questions, but she was shaking like a leaf. Finally, the police completed their forensic investigation and they contacted the coroner's office to pick up the body. The woman was wheeled out on a gurney covered in a crisp white sheet. Her form was outlined perfectly under the sheet. The dips and curves of her body were still and perfect. I felt sad for her and her family, even though I didn't know who she was or where she came from. Though she was gone, the odor of her decomposition remained. The policeman told my Mother how to get rid of the odor in the room — burn coffee beans in a pot over a hot plate.

Burnie, nor my Mother were going near that room. As far as they were concerned, that room could go unoccupied for eternity. As always, the duty of work fell on my lap. I wasn't particularly interested in going into a room where the woman's remains had just been discovered, but if not me, then who? I did as I was instructed and placed the coffee beans in a pot on a hot plate in room #2. The smell of coffee filled the room and the remnants of the woman's demise drifted away with the aroma. Fear had gripped my Mother and Burnie and they stayed up most of that night. I went to bed because I had to go to work the next morning. Twig said originally there was a man and a woman that rented the room, but later three women came and went into the room by themselves. He said he heard someone holler and soon after, only two women came out of room #2. When he was questioned, the officer asked him why he didn't inform my Mother about the woman screaming and he said he was afraid and didn't want to see my Mom get hurt. Twig told the officers he had, in his room, a piece of paper with the license plate number of the car that the women left in. We were all shocked. He had the presence of mind to write down the license plate number! Ultimately, the police were able to find the women and they were convicted of murder and sent to prison. We were told after the trial that the women worked at a convalescent home where the dead woman lived, and they were afraid they were going to get caught because they were using her credit cards. The District Attorney's Office had Twig come to City Hall and honored him for his quick thinking and cracking the case. Twig was given the hat that the District Attorney wore when he was in the service. Marion was so proud of Twig, and so were we. It took four months before Burnie or my Mother went back into that room.

Moving Forward and Not Looking Back

My Mother, Burnie, and I always worked as a team and each owned one-third of the business. My Mother wanted to be fair with all our purchases because we all worked together. We started purchasing single-family homes on the Eastside of town. One large house we converted into a rooming house. We furnished it with used furniture, and I was the one to rent a truck and do the driving when we picked up the pieces. Because Burnie was an exceptional seamstress, she made a lot of my clothes, as well as her own. She loved sewing and made all the curtains in the rooming house. She was also a master at laying tile. My Mother was the banker. She could handle money better than anyone I know. With her sixth-grade education, she could calculate interest and amortization in her head. She was amazing. I was also the painter and I painted all the interiors in all our properties. Sometimes I would leave the Sheriff's Department and go paint an apartment and return the next day until it was finished. I kept my overalls in the trunk of my car so that when I left my job, I could change in my car to be ready to paint at one of our properties. Although we worked hard, my Mother stressed the need for us to have fun. She had taken lessons from her own life and required that we work **AND** play. Burnie took the play part to heart, and I, the work part.

I remember one day when I was around 22 years old, I was painting the exterior of a one-story duplex that we owned. I painted professionally just like my Dad. Some men were across the street drinking and laughing at the girl on the ladder painting the house. They had never seen a girl painting the exterior of a building. Young and sensitive, I started crying and my Mother asked me what was wrong. I told her what the men across the street were saying. It bothered me so much that they didn't think I should be doing what I was doing, just because I was a female. My 22-year-old feelings were hurt and raw. My Mother looked me in the eye and recounted her own experiences with being underestimated. She reminded me of all the times she was told that she couldn't do something because she was female and Black and poor. She demanded that I wipe my tears and get back on that ladder and paint that house. She said, "La-Doris, today they laugh, tomorrow you will laugh." She could see where our life was going, and we couldn't let anything, or anyone deter our progress. She was right.

We continued to purchase houses on the Eastside of town. In the span of a few years, we had amassed several buildings. We were moving forward and not looking back. One day, Burnie told Mom that we needed to look into purchasing properties in better areas. Affluent areas were on the Westside and banks knew that the buying power was on the Westside; however, Black faces weren't always welcomed there. No matter how many properties we owned on the Eastside of town, the banks were hell bent on limiting our access to the Westside. My Mother was unmoved. She had never taken "no" for an answer, and she wasn't going to start now. She instructed us to begin finding properties to purchase on the Westside. We ran into difficulties because we were Black, and realtors were reluctant to show us properties. We often had to lie and say that our White boss was sending us out first to preview them or that we were the housekeepers of the current owners and we had to assess the cleanliness of the home before it was shown to any potential buyers. When we decided on a property, we would enlist our White Jewish friends to assist in the purchase. We didn't need their money, but we did need their white skin to complete the transactions. The DeWald Baum family lived on Beverly Drive. They had always treated us well and we were true family friends. We approached them with the issue surrounding our purchase power and the banks apprehension to issue a loan to Black people. We devised a plan that they would buy the property with our money and then quit claim the deed to us after the closing of Escrow. Three Black women, led by a woman from Troy, Alabama with a sixth-grade education managed to circumvent the blatant racism of a national bank and wealthy property owners and ultimately create a real estate empire right under their noses. To think about it now, I laugh. We did it and they had no idea. My Mother planned years earlier that she wasn't going to be owned by anyone anymore and she relied on her intuition and faith to grow our family business. I became a skilled negotiator and closed deals left and right. Today, I marvel at how far we came starting all over after my Mom and Dad divorced. She held true to her promise that she would recoup everything that she lost. And much like the removal of the stench that permeated room #2, the scent of success was beginning to blow into our lives to remove the smell of divorce and loss.

Although the winds of change were beginning to blow, there would often be a gust that reminded us that racism was alive and well. DeWald told us about a property in Century City for sale and that we should consider buying it. Ever the advocate, DeWald told us about a 13-unit building with fireplaces in each unit. The building also boasted a large swimming pool, floor-to-ceiling windows, and private patios. It sounded magnificent. Before the purchase was final, I took a drive to Century City to look over the building and assess the tenants. I glided through the gates and made my way to the swimming pool where several White residents were sunbathing. Two of the White female residents asked sarcastically whether I was the new owner. I replied, "No. I am a new member of the maintenance crew." They then commented that they knew a woman purchased the building and they thought that she was probably on a cruise somewhere.

After the close of Escrow, I spent a significant amount of time at the Century City building. I would often encounter those two tenants and they were always pleasant enough. Never revealing my identity, the tenants would gift me with used designer clothes. I had no shame in accepting such fine gifts from women who easily believed that I was a member of the maintenance staff, that is, until the *Los Angeles Times* ruined my ruse. There she was, my Mother, in all her finery, standing in front of the McClaney Estate, grinning from ear-to-ear on the front page of the newspaper. It was a proud day for our family, but it was also the day that I stopped getting free designer clothes from those benevolent tenants, and they stopped fueling their White guilt by giving the poor Black girl their hand me downs.

We ran the motel business for ten years and then converted it into a residential care facility serving World War II Veterans and developmentally disabled adults. We had difficulties getting our license. The woman from the licensing bureau told us we had to move from the motel, change all our beds from standard to twin, and she required us to comply with countless other rules. They were endless. We knew that the obstacles in our wake were because the licensing board didn't want Black women to run such a facility. We became exasperated, but undeterred with all the changes we had to do at Flagstone. Each agency came with different rules. And each time, we followed them to the letter.

Two years into the licensing process, we received a letter from the agency stating that they were closing our application. Burnie was furious. Flagstone was compliant in all ways to operate as a residential care facility. She was not going to allow a bunch of White bureaucrats to give us the runaround any longer. She contacted a friend named Ondra Lewis. Ondra knew of the delays and frustrations we were having. She worked for the board of education and had gone through a similar situation with bureaucracy and red tape to get things done in the City of Los Angeles. She said she knew a person that was sharp and could help us re-open our application. He came to the motel and told us he had contacted Sacramento and would walk our papers through the necessary channels. He contacted the licensing manager that closed our application and told her he would be taking over our case. He told her that he was on his way to Sacramento to file a formal complaint about the closing and that she may want to reconsider the viability of our application. She came to Flagstone the next day. When she met us at the door, her mouth dropped. Our facility was beautiful. I think she expected mediocrity and basic furnishings. Instead, she found manicured grounds, beautiful rooms, and stellar staffing. She wanted a reason to uphold her earlier decision, but she found none. There's nothing more satisfying than seeing overt racism die on site. We watched her write the report while gritting her teeth with every stroke of her pen. We bid her farewell as she hopped into her compact Pinto. She pulled out and glared at my Mother's new Mercedes and sped off. Three weeks later our license came in the mail.

We loved the new business. We had prayed about Flagstone's transformation into a facility for Veterans and He gave us exactly what we prayed for. Burnie and I even bought matching beige and white Volkswagen vans to carry our clients around. God had always directed our decisions and Flagstone was no exception. We were helping people who needed our assistance and were able to give them a home. In return, it gave us a steady income along with our rental properties. We provided our guests with three meals a day, social activities, and meetings with social workers once a month for the evaluation of our clients. The residents at Flagstone became our extended family. A special school called Willing Workers was located two blocks from Flagstone and some of our residents attended classes there five days a week to gain a skill or a trade that they could build a future upon. Burnie and I continued our work at Flagstone. We both did most of the cooking along with my Mother and were able to hire custodial personnel to keep our facility clean. As always, I painted rooms after one resident moved out and Burnie made all of the floor repairs when they were needed.

We had worked in the family business for over a decade and although we were successful, my Mother constantly reminded us that college was still calling. No matter our economic or social status, my Mother demanded that we earn a college degree. At our Mother's fervent urging (and occasional threat), Burnie and I decided that it would be in our best interest to go back to college and get our degrees. We knew that our introduction to the world of social services and meeting the requirements for licensing had been through grace. Getting our education would cement our future and we wanted to make sure that no obstacles existed for future licensing requirements. We figured that instead of paying an outside social worker or administrator to come in and do what we knew how to do, we would pay tuition to college to earn the requisite degrees and do the jobs ourselves. We enrolled in a program at the University of Southern California (USC) that offered an extension program from Shaw University, a Historically Black College and University (HBCU) located in Raleigh, North Carolina. Our classes were held at USC, but our bachelor's degree was granted from Shaw. We were adamant that those tuition funds would go directly to Shaw. Our love and admiration for HBCUs was strong then and remains strong today. The program allowed college credit to be awarded for those who had significant work experience in their chosen field of study. I earned a degree in behavioral science and Burnie received a degree in urban planning and development. My Mother was happy that we had received our undergraduate degrees, but she said that she would not stop asking about our education until **AFTER** we received our master's degree.

A year after graduating from Shaw, we began a master's program at Pepperdine University in South Central Los Angeles. We heard about the master's program from Maxine Waters. Her husband had graduated from Pepperdine years before and he spoke highly of the University. Burnie and I attended and earned our master's degrees together. My Mother was finally pleased with our academic progress. She valued education and knew that it was the only thing in life that couldn't be taken away. An educated Black woman could do anything, and she knew it. She would often remind us that even with a PhD we would never be as smart as her. She was right.

Earning a Master's in Public Administration was a highlight in my life. I was working in the field that I loved, with my family, and I had just earned a degree that would propel us even further. I was in the process of applying to doctoral programs when I received a call from Bethune-Cookman University. They wanted to bestow upon me an honorary doctoral degree. I loved learning, but if I could be afforded all the rights and privileges of a PhD without the 4 years of classes and dissertation preparation, I was going to do just that! I walked onto that stage at Bethune-Cookman and received that honorary doctorate in 1988. I was done with school; my Mother's wish had been granted and that is all that mattered. Years later, I further sealed the doctoral deal by receiving another honorary doctoral degree from Shorter College in Little Rock, Arkansas.

We operated Flagstone Guest Haven from 1968 to 1988. Everyone came to Flagstone. Our friends were from the upper echelon of Black society in America and they would come to Flagstone to hang out with the Veterans and eat my Mother's cooking. On any given day, you would see the likes of Wilt Chamberlain, Bill Russell, The Harlem Globe Trotters, Congressman Julian Bond, boxer Archie Moore, Lena Horne, Linda Hopkins, Reverend Ike, The Platters, Marvin Gaye, Lou Rawls, and many others playing ball or barbecuing in the courtyard. It was the hang out spot. My Mother was everyone's mother and she would cook, and they would eat. Everyone loved my Mother because she was like a mother to them. The courtyard at Flagstone was like the playground in Pittsburgh that flanked the projects that we lived in years before and the Bermuda Shorts party at the Lewis Estate. Nothing, yet everything had changed.

Moving to Beverly Drive, Beverlywood

We moved from the motel to an apartment building on Beverly Drive. At the time, I was working at a stock firm in Beverly Hills called Burr Wilson & Company as a teletype operator and was the only Black employee there. I contacted a realtor to inquire about available apartment buildings that were for sale in the Beverly Hills or Beverlywood area. We took four Veterans with us: George Jones, Henry Miller, Ray Marvin, and Louis Whitney. Any government assistance that was available for their relocation was insufficient, so they came with us to our new home on Beverly Drive.

George was special. I tried hard not to play favorites, but George was my favorite. He had suffered the ills of war and mental illness and had been all but abandoned by his family. He was one of the first residents at Flagstone. He was my partner in crime and my constant companion on road trips to Las Vegas. Before he fell ill and age came calling, he would spend his afternoons at Caesar's Palace gambling and eating at the buffets. He was my friend, the older brother I always hoped for, and a staple in our home. When he died, another piece of me died too.

When we decided to move from Flagstone, I contacted the realtor on a sign outside of a building. Her name was Phyllis. I gave her my telephone number in Beverly Hills and told her we were interested in purchasing a building in the Beverly Hills or Beverlywood area of Los Angeles. I also asked that she provide me with as many listings as possible in those areas. If we found something that we liked, I would contact her directly for a showing. I had learned long ago that relationships were the bedrock of success. My Mother's relationship with Betty Lewis, her parent's relationship with Mr. Davis, my grandparent's relationship with the community for the hog roasts – relationships often trumped education, information, or location. When we found the Beverly Drive property, we loved it and immediately called Phyllis.

Phyllis and I had never met in person. We had only communicated on the phone. For several weeks, we talked and spoke about the specifications that we were looking for in a property. She was diligent in getting back to me with listings that were on the Multi Listing Service (MLS) database, as well as those that she had inside knowledge about and hadn't yet made it on the list. The MLS is the clearinghouse for real estate sales and the commonplace for investors to learn about hot listings that are available, but having a realtor in the know about listings that were upcoming and not yet listed on the MLS, was the Holy Grail of real estate investment. The Beverly Drive property was one of those properties. We got wind of it being for sale and Phyllis and I decided to meet at the property. Since we had never met, I asked her to describe herself. She said she was Jewish, short, heavy, and would be wearing a blue dress. I said I was medium height and would be wearing a blue dress too. We were scheduled to meet at Beverly Drive at 2:00 PM. Me, Burnie, and my Mother arrived at the building at 1:00 PM to sit and observe the area and the residents.

At 2:20 PM, Phyllis pulled up and you could see the surprised look on her face. She couldn't hide it. You would've thought she saw a ghost, or at least one that had a Black face and wore a blue dress. We got out of the car and introduced ourselves. When we arrived at the front door of the Beverly Drive property, the granddaughter of the owner opened the door and screamed. She was 15. My Mother, sister, and I looked at each other and smiled. We viewed the apartment on the first floor and when we arrived on the second floor, the granddaughter had the biggest picture of Jimmy Hendricks with his untamed afro filling the poster on her wall. I realized then that White people want our culture but not us. The owner and the broker disappeared. I told my Mother and Burnie to keep talking as I walked backward to listen in on their conversation. I saw the broker explaining to the owner that she was unaware that we were Black. They couldn't hide it. They were shocked when I walked up and explained that we were prepared to make an offer to buy the building at full asking price. They scoffed in disbelief. The only caveat was that we wanted to see all of the units before the purchase. We returned several days later to view the entire building. The broker said we didn't need to pay full price. We could make a "more affordable" offer instead. We respectfully declined her advice. We weren't going to give them any excuse to back out of the deal.

The down payment requested was thirty percent instead of the normal twenty percent. We bought that building for $99,500. We agreed to pay the thirty percent because we knew the game and we weren't going to give the owners any room to back out of the deal. If they asked for forty percent, we would have paid that. Their attempts to outsmart us yielded no fruit. We were ready, willing, and able to comply with their requests because we wanted the building and not getting it wasn't an option. When we went to open Escrow, we went with our attorney Jerry Rosen. When he read the Covenants, Conditions, and Restrictions (CC&Rs) papers that accompany most real estate transactions, he said, "What the hell is this?" The CC&Rs specified the property was never to be sold to "Blacks, Mexicans, or any other minority." More blatant racism that had reared its ugly head, not just in words or deeds, but on paper, in front of us, spelled out with unmistakable language. We were forbidden from buying the property simply because we were Black and our Jewish lawyer (who incidentally would have been forbidden from buying the property as well) was livid. We looked at everyone at the table and smiled. Instead of using cash to open Escrow, I suggested we put up our stocks and keep our liquid capital in the bank, drawing interest until the close of Escrow. The Escrow officer said she had not done that in the past. I explained to her that we could see what the market value was, and we would be willing to put up over twenty percent stock for our retainer. Their faces dropped. They couldn't figure out how a Black woman knew anything about stocks or interest or real estate investments. I'm sure when we left that meeting, they were gob smacked and called me names. What they thought of me was of no consequence. We wanted the building and we were going to buy it no matter what.

We purchased the apartment building and requested that all the tenants move because we wanted to take full occupancy of the building. Fifty years ago, you could make that kind of request. Now, that would never be permitted unless you paid the tenants a relocation fee. The White folks in the area were astonished. They knew that Black people had purchased the building and the news of the purchase spread like wildfire. They would walk up and down the street peeking in to see us like we were a new attraction at an amusement park! We were the first Blacks to buy property in Beverlywood. The year was 1969. White people couldn't understand how Blacks, let alone Black women, were able to buy an entire building, but we did. As always, my Mother worked her magic and we had the most beautiful apartment building in the area. We met a gentleman named George Stern whose father had a fabric store in the Downtown Los Angeles area called Stern Draperies. We explained to him that my Mother wanted velvet drapes made to match her magenta walls. We gave him a paint bucket with the color, and he matched the draperies to perfection. George continued to make all our draperies for our apartment buildings. We became personal friends and are friends to this day. When we would leave our building, we would leave all the windows open. When we returned, neighbors were in our yard looking inside the windows at our apartments because they were showstoppers. When we returned home unexpectedly, they would look sheepish and say we had the most beautiful apartments they had ever seen. We laughed and thanked God again for his goodness.

My Mother, grandmother, and Georgia Mae occupied the two-story front unit. Burnie and I shared the two-story unit next to theirs. We brought four of our Veterans from Flagstone to live in a two-bedroom two-bath unit, and we kept another two-bedroom, two-bath unit vacant for guests when they visited. Beverly Drive was now home.

Burnie was Miss Personality and she knew **everyone** in Los Angeles. We started having beautiful parties in the rear of the building inviting our friends. The neighbors would peek out of their windows in the building next to ours and they would often bring their friends to the window to watch as well. They had never seen Black folks live a life like we had. Celebrities, politicians, and the who's who of Los Angeles came to our parties and our neighbors had a front row window seat. Our guests were treated to valet parking, live music, and plenty of fantastic food. Everyone was dressed like they were going to the Academy Awards.

Welcome to Holmby Hills

After living on Beverly Drive for six and a half years, Burnie and I convinced our Mother that it was time for us to move to a home where we could entertain our friends as we did in Pittsburgh. She was agreeable and I started house hunting in Beverly Hills. Burnie didn't like house hunting but said that once we found a house we liked she would come and check it out and give her approval. That was Burnie's way - she didn't like the hunt, but she enjoyed making the deals. She enjoyed the parties, but never the plans. She liked building business relationships, but not the grunt work it took to maintain the business.

Mother and I loved the hunt. We spent weeks looking in people's homes because we were, well, nosey. We would visit the homes that were for sale in Beverly Hills and admire the furnishings to get our own design ideas. We ventured out to fine furniture stores to get a sense of what was in style and what was considered timeless interior décor since we managed to keep much of the furniture that we had at the Lewis Estate. Looking at the furniture, I would find myself reminiscing about my family and how it had been broken so many years before. The relationship with my Dad was strained. When he divorced my Mother, he divorced Burnie and I as well. My heart hurt, but I didn't let that dictate my life. Somehow, chairs, setees, tables, and sofas held all those memories of pain and hope.

We spent a tremendous amount of time looking for a new home. There were no homes in the area that we desired and could afford or that met our specifications. Burnie had a broker take us to Holmby

Hills. I couldn't figure out where Holmby Hills was. Burnie said to me, "La-Doris do you remember where we play tennis in Bel Air, and drive down Beverly Glen Boulevard? The houses on the East side of the street is where Holmby Hills starts." Looking back, I'm not surprised that Burnie knew about Holmby Hills and its notable residents. She was, after all, the social butterfly who ran in very wealthy circles. Holmby Hills was, and still is, one of the top four, most expensive and exclusive enclaves in Southern California. Burnie had fallen in love with two houses on Beverly Glen Boulevard. She would point them out each time we passed by the homes. We settled on one of the two houses. A beautiful estate right on Beverly Glen, close to the world-famous Sunset Boulevard.

At the time of purchasing the home on Beverly Glen, we were in Escrow with a twenty-four-unit apartment building. I asked my Mother if she thought we would be able to purchase both properties at the same time as these two purchases were the largest to date. I'm not even sure why I asked her, because I already knew the answer. She assured me that both purchases would go through and I believed her. We closed both deals within two days of each other. My Mother said we needed the twenty-four-unit building so we could continue our lifestyle. The bank didn't know whether the money that they saw in Escrow was for the house or the apartment building. I never told them. Our income was sufficient to pull off the deal. To ensure that our monthly financial plan would work, we delayed our property taxes for two months. We spent most of our funds buying the properties and things were lean until the following month when the rents were paid, and the money rolled back around. To that end, we didn't have money to hire a large moving company to move our furniture into our new home. Burnie and I asked our friends to help. One of our friends had worked for a moving company and was very knowledgeable about moving furniture. I was too since I spent time in Pittsburgh moving my Mother's furniture after the divorce. Burnie's friend told us what size truck to rent, and we all met at the apartment building to start our move.

We did not sell our apartment building on Beverly Drive. The neighbors were shocked! We loved Beverly Drive and wanted to keep it and rent it out as income property. I still own that building today. Here we were, owning an apartment building and several other properties, and now we were moving to Holmby Hills, and we didn't have to sell one thing to buy it. Moving day was an exciting day. We were all dressed in our work clothes and ready for a hard day's work. The previous owners had left the house in excellent condition. All we needed to do was some interior painting because you could see where they had removed pictures off the walls.

When we arrived, Mom knew exactly where she wanted her furniture to be placed. I asked that no furniture be placed against the walls because I was the one who was going to paint the entire interior of the house. I needed enough room to get behind the furniture to paint the walls. Some friends worked in the linen closet, some in the kitchen, some in the library, and some hung clothes in the closets. It was teamwork and we were so grateful to have so many friends willing to help us. And there I was again, bucket in my left hand and brush in my right. I painted the entire house, by myself. Every room, bathroom, hall, nook, and cranny were painted by me. While we were moving in, Mom cooked a big meal for us, and it became a huge party. Although we were all exhausted, it felt so good because we had accomplished the impossible. It was a lot of work. You never know how much you have until you decide to move. Without our friends, there would have been no way for us to move our belongings to Holmby Hills.

Living in Holmby Hills was fun. Most people thought that we were celebrities. Seeing Black people in that area was like seeing a unicorn. We would watch as tour buses passed by our home. Spectators would peek into the large electric gates when they opened to see if they could see who lived inside. Even the postman was perplexed by us living there. Many times, when packages were delivered, the postman would enter the gates, drive through the circular driveway, knock on the door, and was met with a Black face. He would say that only the owner could sign for the package. We smiled, signed, and closed the door and laughed out loud. I never felt like I had to prove myself to anyone. If the postman thought that I was the help, that was fine. I knew I was the owner.

There was one occasion where we had returned from church one Sunday morning. We pulled up to the house in my Mother's black and white Rolls Royce and noticed that the side door was wide open. We had learned from the Flagstone room #2 incident that we were not going to enter the house. Instead, we called the Bel Air Police Department. They came immediately and entered the house, looked around, and told us it was okay to enter. As they were leaving one officer turned and said to us, "This is a beautiful home and you girls certainly keep it immaculate. The owners should be proud of you." We smiled and thanked the officers and walked into our home. We laughed about it. I couldn't believe the level of racism and ignorance that they exhibited. My grandmother stood with us on the driveway and she was 95 years old, balancing on a cane.

In Holmby Hills, we rekindled our Beverly Drive and Lewis Estate tradition of having incredible parties. Most political people running for office used our home for their fundraisers. Burnie knew them all and they all came. The parties were very elegant, and people wore their finest. Everyone who was anyone wanted to party at The McClaney Estate. That's what we named the house on Beverly Glen. They looked forward to coming to The McClaney Estate. The mansion was beautifully decorated and full of catered food, wonderful music, and we routinely provided our guests with valet parking. We had our own Estate and it was ours in perpetuity. Having this lifestyle and this home caused some difficulty with some of the people we had to do business with. The jealousy couldn't be hidden. Holmby Hills took me right back to my high school days where people loved what I had but not who I was. As I did in those early days, I did not hold a grudge. I simply did my best and kept stepping.

We moved into our home in June 1975. I remarried in May 1976. That marriage ended in 1980 in divorce. All I can say is thank God I had a pre-nuptial agreement. I was grateful to have a document protecting my finances and properties in place at the time of our marriage, at the off chance it didn't work. It didn't. I was determined not to lose everything like my Mother did when she and my Father divorced. I lost nothing. I was smart and I listened.

In 1984, Burnie suggested that we create an annual party to celebrate the goodness of God in our lives. It was to be a Gospel Songfest at the house. We would invite everyone to come to sit outside in the driveway, listen to live gospel entertainment, and then continue worship with a guest speaker. The party was simply to praise and honor God. We thought this was an excellent idea, so we enlisted the services of a gentleman that was an artist at Motown Records and a minister named Frank Wilson. We invited him because he had a church and was a well-loved, known personality in the Black faith community. He was delighted and invited members of his church, New Dawn. He partnered with other pastors and they invited their members as well. He brought choirs, musicians, and he selected Minister Chuck Singleton to bring the Word through preaching.

The long circular driveway was adorned with crisp white chairs with soft pillowy cushions. The perimeter of the pool deck was transformed into a large buffet and the center of the terrace became the stage. One thousand people attended the first Gospel Songfest. The event was held every third Saturday in August, turning the McClaney Estate into a mega church. Our neighbors were blessed with song and worship. I have always known the power of God, but on one occasion He moved in such a way that my neighbor and owner of the Playboy Mansion, the late Hugh Hefner, along with several of his Playboy Bunnies, stood near the exit gate listening to the music with hands lifted high. God is real. For 27 years we entertained over 45,000 people at the Gospel Songfest. It was, and remains, one of Burnie's greatest contributions to our family legacy.

McClaney Estate, as well as our other properties, have always been home. They were never simply houses or dwellings. Even then, they served as havens for those that needed a place to rest and revitalize their lives. On occasion, we would host people who had fallen on hard times. Countless celebrities and dignitaries rested their heads in our homes when things had shifted dramatically in their lives. Divorce, job loss, abuse, and financial ruin were the undercurrents in the lives of those who appeared to have it all. We never shamed anyone, nor did we divulge their secrets. Rather, we provided them with a home, food, and dignity as they sorted out the complexities of their lives. We had earned so much that it was only right to give to others. In fact, the only reason we had so much is because we had given so much to others.

Our homes were open to everyone. At one point my uncle Lewis (known as Tommie Lee) was having real difficulty with his breathing and was in and out of the hospital. His doctor advised him he needed to relocate to either Florida or California because he had a severe case of Asthma and the air quality in those states would help alleviate his ailments. He decided to come to California because of his sister and he knew she would take care of him. He moved to California and stayed with us at the motel for six months. In that time, he secured a job and soon after, sent for his wife Clara Mae and their three children. They all stayed at the motel and that extended our family. Eventually, he made enough money to purchase a home in Los Angeles, with the assistance of my Mother. She cosigned on the property and provided additional funds to purchase the house, which he later paid back in full. In ironic fashion, my Mother had been the Betty Lewis in my uncle's life.

Death of Burnie

My sister Burnie was my best friend. We didn't always agree on everything, but she was my sister. We were very different people, but our love conquered every disagreement. By 1985, our lives at the McClaney Estate was well settled. We had acquired additional properties across the country, and we were financially solvent. We were at the point where our money was working for us. We still worked hard to maintain our real estate portfolio, but we were no longer pressured to build. It was like climbing a mountain. We expended so much time, energy, money, and effort in the prior 20 years and now, we could stand at the summit and bask in the glow of our success.

My Mother had learned how to be a wealthy woman. She had beautiful cars and some designer clothes. She had also adopted my practice of taking weekly trips to the salon to be pampered and primped. On one of our weekly salon trips in 1985, as our nails were being painted and our hair styled, God was manifesting a new reality and our lives were about to be forever changed.

Sitting in the stylist's chair, I received a call from Burnie. She knew me and my Mother's routine, so it was easy for her to find us. On the other end of the phone, I heard my sister crying. She stated that she had just left the doctor's office and had been given results of her checkup. Cancer. Lung Cancer. That word reverberated in my ear like a bell. I thought I heard her wrong. Cancer? My sister has Cancer? My sister has Lung Cancer? My heart stopped for a moment. I'm not sure what the rest of the phone call was about, but as I spoke to Burnie, I

123

was watching my Mother with her trademark toothy grin, as she giggled and cooed with her stylist. I was about to change her life forever. I was charged, again, to do the hard work. I had to tell my Mother that her eldest daughter, the one who hiked the Alabama woods in the dark of night with her, the one who was the life of the party, the one who found Beverly Glen, the one who was the brightest light in our family — Burnie, her daughter had Lung Cancer. When I told my Mother about Burnie, she was still. She didn't yell or run or even shake. She was stiff as a board and still. We were in complete shock because Burnie had never shared that she was sick. She knew for a long time that she had Cancer, but we had no idea. Even though Burnie was social, she kept private matters private. She said that she kept her illness quiet because she didn't want to worry Mother or me. I was devastated. I didn't know she was sick. She kept it a secret because she didn't want us to hurt. She wanted to be quiet.

My Mother and I left the salon immediately. We called Burnie to let her know that we were coming to be with her at her home. She asked that we come later because she wanted to rest. She assured us that she would call us when she woke up from her slumber. We obliged and went home. Burnie wasn't living at McClaney Estate. She had moved from the house and was living in one of our apartment buildings that was once owned by Bing Crosby. It was a four-story building with an elevator. She had her own apartment on the second floor and had been living there for several years while me, my Mother, and grandmother occupied McClaney Estate on Beverly Glen. She called us later that evening and said she was feeling much better. We were in constant contact with her. Several days later she was on the telephone talking to my Mother and said she had to hang up because she was having difficulty breathing. She said that she was going to go outside for some fresh air. My Mother's instincts kicked in and she summoned me to drive her to Burnie's apartment. We left immediately.

By the time we arrived at the apartment building, an ambulance was already outside.

Red lights flooded our gaze as I parked the car. I ran across the street straight to the ambulance driver. I explained that we owned the building and my sister was having difficulty breathing when she spoke to my Mother earlier. I told him that my sister had been recently diagnosed with Lung Cancer and that a team of horses was the only thing that would prevent me from getting to my sister's apartment. He told me to stand next to the building and brace myself. I explained to him that my name is La-Doris McClaney and I don't take "no" for an answer. I told him that he was either going to let me up to her apartment or he would have to render aid to himself in that ambulance. My words were enough, and I rushed to her door. Before I could get up the steps fully, I saw my beloved sister laying still right inside the front door of the building. I became hysterical. They swiftly covered my beloved sister's lifeless body with a crisp white sheet. She lay there, still, quiet, and alone. I had fought for her my entire life, but this day, as I looked at the dips and curves of her lifeless form under that crisp white sheet, her greatest fight, that she secretly fought alone, was over. The ambulance driver had followed me up the stairs and I heard him say, "I am so sorry…she expired."

She had died right in the entrance hall of her apartment building. I stood in total shock and disbelief. My shock had to be tempered because my Mother was across the street in her car, waiting for me. I composed myself as best as I could and walked to my Mother. I think, even before I uttered a word, she knew. My Mother knew that her daughter was gone. "Mommy? Burnie is gone…she died." My Mother almost fainted in the street. As her knees buckled her soul did too. She was inconsolable. Her crying was carnal and raw. Her grief came from the depths of her gut and the sound that emitted from her tore into the stillness of the moment. I asked a friend to take her to Flagstone, which was only three miles from the apartment building. Flagstone was always home. There, she could be with staff members at the facility and I would come after all the arrangements were made.

They wheeled my beloved Burnie's body out of the building and to a waiting hearse to transport her to Harrison and Ross Mortuary. We were friends with the mortuary owners, and they came forthwith to tend to Burnie. The mortuary staff waited patiently for Burnie's doctor, Dr. Madison Richardson, to release her body. While Dr. Richardson specializes in Otolaryngology, he was Burnie's doctor. Dr. Richardson is a graduate of Howard University and has been Board Certified for more than 50 years, receiving countless accolades in Cancer research. He was shocked when I called him with my urgent request. I wanted Burnie to be cared for with delicate loving hands and I knew that Harrison and Ross would do just that. I didn't want her taken to the morgue — she deserved every ounce of attention and care and I didn't want her in a place with strangers, amongst the masses of bodies. I wanted her with people that she knew and loved. As we awaited the documents from Dr. Richardson, a sea of people from the neighborhood began to gather. As the tenants started coming home from work, they had to be redirected to enter the building from the rear. They all were in complete shock. They loved our beloved Burnie and, like us, they had no idea she was having any health issues. She masked her illness well. She maintained her gregarious, social self. She was full of energy and was friendly even on the day she died. Her illness was her own personal secret that she kept.

Even writing this now, my heart is still broken. I weep when I think about that day. I never thought I would have to live without Burnie. After some friends were notified, Mother wanted me to call Dr. Leroy Vaughn. Dr. Vaughn was like a son to her. He was in Europe vacationing with his entire family. When he received the word that Burnie had passed, he cut his European vacation short and immediately caught a flight back to Los Angeles to be with my Mother. This man, Dr. Vaughn, was a world-renowned physician who graduated Phi Beta Kappa from Morehouse College. He completed his medical degree at the University of Vienna in Austria. This man, who was a Harvard trained Ophthalmologist, who was the recipient of countless awards including the prestigious Franklin C. McClean Award for being the most outstanding medical student in the nation, left his European vacation to sit with my Mother, to pray with and for her. I will always be eternally grateful for his act of kindness and his family's sacrifice during our time of tremendous loss.

Burnie's death immediately went over the airwaves and people started calling from all over the country. We had to hire security because so many people began to come to the house to offer their condolences. We ultimately decided to open the guest house that sits below the main house to allow people to congregate, relax, and reflect on the beautiful life that was just lost. We kept my Mother inside to grieve privately. A dear friend of the family named John was a chef and he prepared all the food and put it in the guest house for people to eat when they came to pray, sit, and grieve.

That day was also the beginning of my Mother's demise. She was never the same. No Mother wants to bury their child, and my Mother was no exception. I can't begin to describe the depth and breadth of our pain. Knowing that Burnie was safely at Harrison and Ross, I stepped back into working. This time, however, I was making funeral arrangements for my sister. My Mother couldn't bear to do it. She neither had the desire, nor the drive to do much more than take a few sips of water and sleep. Each passing moment, I thought I was going to lose her too. Dr. Randall Maxey came and attended to her.

Dr. Maxey, a noted Nephrologist who studied at Howard University, focuses his efforts on the correlation between coronary artery disease in the prevention of kidney disease. He was once the president of the National Medical Association, the country's largest professional organization for American doctors. Dr. Maxey was Godsent.

Twenty-five years before Burnie's death, my Mother had purchased plots at Forest Lawn Cemetery at Hollywood Hills for all of us. She purchased five plots, one each for Georgia Mae, Burnie, herself, Grannie, and me. The cemetery gave me all the information I needed to bury Burnie. Burnie was a member of Science of Mind and belonged to Founders Church. I contacted the church and some of our friends came to the house to attend to all the phone calls and to do her program.

As we all sat in the kitchen the day before the funeral, my Daddy came around the corner from the butler's pantry and settled his stance in front of the sink. To my utter shock and surprise, there he stood, older and careworn. I had called him to tell him about Burnie, but I didn't think he was going to come to celebrate her life. We hadn't seen him in 20 years. This was the first-time my Mother had seen my Father since leaving Pittsburgh. He and I had spoken, but only on the telephone. My Mother hadn't heard his voice in two decades. By this time, he had remarried and was still living at the Lewis Estate. He reached out and gave me a hug and I melted into his arms. I was concerned about my Mother's reaction upon seeing him as she sat in the kitchen at the table when he rounded the corner. They locked eyes, he bent over and kissed her on the cheek, but my Mother did not react. They never discussed the divorce. This season wasn't about any of that. It was about Burnie. My Mother insisted that I take him on a tour of the properties that we had purchased. She wanted him to see what she and her daughters were able to accomplish despite his absence.

He was speechless, but somehow mustered breathlessly the word, "beautiful" as we passed each building. At the time, all our properties bore the name *McClaney Properties*. His Father's surname – our name – was printed boldly on the signage. As he viewed them from the passenger's seat of my Mother's Rolls Royce, he realized that she had done the impossible without him. The next day he attended the funeral, but he returned to the airport and flew back to Pittsburgh immediately following the service. I hardly noticed his departure because I was preoccupied with making sure my Mother was alright. My Mother's health was never the same after Burnie's death and I watched her closely as it declined.

Burnie had a huge service. The church was packed to every corner and was standing room only. People were everywhere. It appeared that the entire world came to celebrate her life. The one person who was there as she entered the world, was just unable to be there when she left — my Mother. She was simply not physically able to attend the service. The crowd at the church had begun to gather before we left the house. Bill Withers, a famous singer, songwriter and composer, came to the house to be with my Mother. Great friends and several other people were at the house with her too.

Dr. Maxey contacted a private home health agency to come and evaluate my Mother's health. Dorothy Ellis was the owner and she arrived at our home every day at 5:30 in the morning to check my Mother's vitals. Dorothy was a registered nurse who earned a Bachelor of Science degree in Nursing from the University of Central Arkansas. When she was just 24 years old, she started a home healthcare business that provided nursing care to private clients. She was the perfect fit for my Mother. She was a go-getter who had created her own fortune, just like my Mom. They spoke the same language. More than anything, though, she loved my Mother. She cared for her with such tenderness and grace. My Mother constantly asked Dorothy how much money she owed her for her services. Dorothy never accepted a dime from us. She cared for her out of sheer love and devotion.

Life was different without Burnie. I managed to continue to work at Flagstone and keep the apartment buildings going. I will never forget people coming to me saying that Burnie owed them money or Burnie said they could have her jewelry or fur coats. My response was always the same, "She's at Forest Lawn Cemetery, feel free to go collect what you were promised." Burnie gave away a lot more than she owed anyone. She was a giver and people took advantage of her, even after she died. People recognized her good heart and generous spirit and often exploited her. Never me, I wasn't the one. Many times, I would tell Burnie that people gather around her because she was a McClaney and knew everyone. Personally, I think they just used her. My Mother decided to sell the apartment building that Burnie lived in. It was just too painful to enter that four-story apartment building without her. The building was sold, along with several other properties that we owned. From the proceeds, we selected 13 charitable organizations to donate millions of dollars in Burnie's name.

Former Mayor of Los Angeles, Tom Bradley, who was like a step-father to me, opened the tower in the Los Angeles City Hall to honor my Mother and me. It was called "A Celebration of Giving." It was a wonderful event and we were so honored to be recognized. As joyous as the day was, it was bittersweet. My Mother's health was failing fast and she even had difficulty walking. She had to be pushed in a wheelchair. A famous artist painted a portrait of Burnie and gave it to my Mother that day. It was so beautiful. My Mother graciously accepted the gift, but her heart broke looking into the eyes of her daughter. I too was in pain. Pain at the loss of my sister and pain as I watched my Mother's health slowly decline. When Burnie died, a part of my Mother died too. And a part of me also. I began cooking special dishes for my Mother to bring her a bit of joy. Food always made her happy. She enjoyed eating and I tried to keep her entertained, but the loss of Burnie had robbed her of true joy. My beloved Mother, my grandmother, and I spent our days quiet and unsure what the future held. We reminisced about Burnie and talked about all the funny things she did. We laughed and cried a lot. We knew that life was never going to be the same and that we were about to enter yet another new world. Little did I know that I was going to live in it alone.

From Sixth Grade to Honorary Doctorate

My Mother never attended high school, let alone college. She was forced to drop out of school in the sixth grade so that she could contribute to the family by working in the fields picking cotton. She was a hard worker all of her life. She didn't idolize many, but she admired people who had a strong work ethic. One person that she often mentioned was Dr. Mary McLeod Bethune. She and Dr. Bethune were kindred spirits. They both built their fortunes selling sweet potato pies, both learned the lessons of hard work while working in the fields picking cotton, and both gave to the Black community to ensure academic and social success. My Mother always had an affinity for Dr. Bethune's story because it paralleled her own.

My Mother wanted to visit the university named in honor of the woman she admired so deeply. Located in Daytona Beach, Florida, Bethune-Cookman University is an HBCU that was founded by Dr. Bethune in 1904. It was originally the Daytona Educational and Industrial Training School for Negro Girls, which later merged with Cookman Institute for Boys, and renamed Daytona Cookman Collegiate Institute. Bethune-Cookman University now sits on 82 acres and has educated millions of scholars. During my Mother's visit there in 1984, she was given the honor of planting a tree on campus. Little did she know, the seedling that she planted then, would become like the cotton seed from Troy and yield a harvest of education and service. The tree, over time, much like my family, would grow strong and wide, providing safe cover and nourishment to a multitude of students.

This offering further manifested in 1986 when my Mother was again invited to the University and was bestowed an honorary doctorate degree for her extensive real estate portfolio and philanthropic endeavors. When she asked the University President, Dr. Oswald Bronson, what an honorary doctorate meant, he said, "You will have all of the rights and privileges of any doctorate degree recipient. Graduate students receive their doctorate after extensive study in their chosen discipline. You are receiving this because of your knowledge, through practical life experience outside of college." She was so proud and honored because college was the one thing that escaped her. Nothing was more important to her than Burnie and I receiving our college degrees. After the ceremony, she let out a hearty laugh and started calling herself Dr. McClaney around the house. Here she was, Eula, with a sixth-grade education, with "Dr." in front of her name. The crop continued to bear fruit when I became a member of the Board of Trustees at Bethune-Cookman University, serving for three terms. Prior to concluding my final term of service, the University President honored me by placing my name on a large building on campus. They named the building the *Dr. La-Doris McClaney School of Performing Arts and Communication*. I had never seen my name placed on such a large building. When I left the Board, I was nominated and elected as Trustee Emeritus. As I left the ceremony, I reflected upon the seeds planted by my mother while I found shade under the tree.

In 1986, I pledged Delta Sigma Theta Sorority, Incorporated. The Century City Chapter invited me to membership and I happily obliged. Delta Sigma Theta is the second Greek sorority established for college educated Black women. The Sorority was founded in 1913 on the campus of Howard University in Washington, D.C. on three basic principles: scholarship, public service, and sisterhood. After our initiation ceremony, a party was given for new members. One of my new sorors, Dr. Jacki Scott, was accompanied by her brother, Tommy

Parker, Jr. The buzz at the party was all about her brother Tommy and you could feel the pulse of energy shift when he walked into the room. Jacki was very nonchalant about it all. Tommy was her brother, and she was unmoved by all the attention that he was receiving. She brought him to the party because she didn't want to attend alone, and she needed a dance partner. Tommy was the perfect guest.

Tommy is a six foot-two-inch-tall, very handsome man who seemed to glide when he walked. He wore his hair parted down the middle with deep waves on each side. The whispers around the room suggested that his hair was a process, a chemical treatment that some Black people use to straighten their hair. He was a great dancer and such a good looking fellow. All the women were looking at him, but he was looking at me.

After the party, my Mother and I along with a friend named Lil Neville went to Honolulu, Hawaii for two weeks. We both needed to get away and relax after Burnie's death. Before we left on our trip, the 100 Black Men of Los Angeles was hosting a grand ball. The 100 Black Men is a national charitable organization whose mission is to educate and mentor African American children and teens. This party was **THE** party to attend. The proceeds went to the organization in an effort to continue their important work in the Black community, but it was also the party where you could find the upper echelon of Black people in Los Angeles. It was a highly coveted, exclusive, invitation-only event. I didn't have a date, and I knew everyone who was anyone would be in attendance. I asked Jacki if she thought her brother would attend the party with me. She said she would ask him. To my delight, he said yes. When we walked into the party, a hush fell over the entire room. He was handsome and I was gorgeous! The men were wondering how he snagged me, and the women were wondering how I snagged him. I never answered their inquiries. I just smiled giving no details and danced the night away. I felt on top of the world and happy for the first time since I lost Burnie.

Tommy and I have continued dating since that night in 1986. He continues to be my beloved, and even as I enter my 83rd year of life, he is still the cream in my coffee. He came into my life at a critical time and he has been my rock ever since. A month later, we attended a party at Mayor Bradley's home and people still couldn't figure out who this handsome man was. It was whispered that he was my trophy for only a couple of weeks. Boy have we proved many people wrong.

Dr. Mildred Singleton was a renowned Ophthalmologist living in Detroit, Michigan. My Mother and I met her while she was studying at Stanford University. She invited us to Detroit, to the opening of the Wright Museum where we anticipated meeting Mrs. Rosa Parks. She was a close friend of Dr. Charles Wright. Dr. Wright was also a physician and was opening an African American museum in Detroit. He was having a large fundraiser and Mildred invited Mother and I to come and be a part of the opening. My Mother was also invited by the Detroit City Council to receive an award for her contributions to the 13 charities she supported. Although we lived in California, my Mother had become well known across the country. We attended the ceremony, and my Mother and I had the privilege of meeting Mrs. Parks.

Mrs. Parks was working part-time for Congressman John Conyers. She told my Mother about the difficulty she was having going to work riding on the bus. My Mother couldn't believe that Rosa Parks lived in Detroit, Michigan where Ford produced cars and she did not have a car. What was more shocking was that Congressman Conyers didn't make provisions for her to have a car. This pillar of Civil Rights and the Mother of the Movement still caught a bus to and from work. Astonishing! We couldn't let that be part of her great legacy.

We met a wonderful woman named Rose Reese who had a beauty salon called Someplace Special and explained Mrs. Parks' transportation dilemma. Rose said she would open her shop with her hairstylists. They would do hair and give makeovers and instead of receiving payment, all the proceeds would go toward the purchase of a car for Mrs. Parks. One of the stylists, Ikie Heard, worked and participated along with other salon operators to spearhead the campaign to collect funds. Before the commencement of the festivities, Ikie invited all of us to her home for dinner. There we sat, in the presence of a Civil Rights icon, supping on cornbread, greens, smothered chicken, and gravy. The truth of the matter was that Mrs. Parks was just like my Mother and other women of that era – down-home women who could sit with heads of state discussing politics and social issues, and on the same day shuck corn on a porch or hand roll dough for peach cobbler all while reminiscing about the old days in the fields. They were true renaissance women. That day in Detroit, Ikie prepared a wonderful meal that rendered us stuffed and gleeful. To this day, Ikie is still cooking. She now lives in Las Vegas. Periodically, Esther Alexander, Norma Archie, and Zelma Willette, who are childhood friends of mine from Pittsburgh, join me at my home in Los Angeles. We call ourselves the Golden Girls too, and Ikie has become a member and the resident chef. The richness of our friendship is worth its weight in gold. This group of friends of mine always enjoy when I entertain them at my home. I cook. Ikie cooks. We eat.

The next day, the campaign to raise funds for the car was announced on the radio and the weekend of the benefit was a huge success. People came from everywhere to give money in support of the effort. When the money was totaled, it was significantly less than what was needed to buy a new car. Mother and I donated the extra amount needed to ensure that Mrs. Parks could buy a new car and drive herself to work. We couldn't believe a woman that had done so much for the Black community was still riding the bus 20 years after that fateful day when she refused to yield to the racist practices in Montgomery. We were honored to ensure that she was always going to ride in the front seat.

December 17, 1987

Death of My Mother

On December 17, 1987, two years after Burnie's death, my Mother died of a heart attack at Flagstone Guest Haven sitting in her Rolls Royce. Because this pain is still so deep, I have to express it in this very matter-of-fact way. Reflecting on her death has tapped into areas of my soul that I closed years ago. I had to continue to work, and work is how I coped with her death.

My Mother loved sitting in her Rolls, taking naps while I was in the office at Flagstone taking care of the daily business. She had purchased her Rolls Royce and paid cash for it when she turned 65 years old and said that she would use her social security check to put gas in it. She spent many days sitting in the car listening to music and just remembering her life in Troy. I imagine her thoughts were full of irony. There she'd sit on leather seats stuffed with the softest cotton, remembering that her marred hands once picked those fluffy mounds to provide for her family. The skins of the hogs that were slaughtered for meals felt eerily similar to the Connolly leather that was pulled tight and handsewn to the steel framed seats. In the summer, she would turn on the air conditioning and feel the cool breeze on her face which reminded her of the cold winds of those Pittsburgh winters as she made pie after pie for sale.

Her naps and sits in the Rolls were a daily occurrence. On that fateful day, there was no alarm when a staff member saw her sitting still in the driver's seat of her car. After an hour or so, something rang different about her position. She wasn't upright as she had always been but slumped in a contorted manner that seemed unnatural. A staff member noticed her in the seat and went dutifully to check on her. As he approached the car, he knew something was very wrong. Her eyes were fixed, and her chest was heaving. He ran back to the office to inform another staff member that he believed that Big Mama was having a heart attack. The staff member came to get me from the office and told me what was happening. I dropped what I was doing, and I ran from the office to the parking lot where my Mother sat, struggling to stay alive. When I opened the car door, I immediately realized that my Mother was gasping for breath. A staff member tore her from the car, and I began administering CPR. I know that I was moving fast, but everything was going in slow motion. Like those moments in an action movie at the height of the action and the film slows down to show the gravity of the explosion or car crash. That is what that moment looked like. As I feverishly huffed and puffed into her body, I felt her life slipping away. I took bigger and deeper breaths and pumped them into her lungs. I recalled how she huffed and puffed with me in her belly as she hiked through those Alabama woods when she was eight and a half months pregnant with me. Why couldn't I save her as she had saved me? Why wasn't my breath enough? Mid puff, I called to the staff to call an ambulance and Dr. Maxey. I needed my Mother to get emergency medical attention. My breath was not enough. I needed to save her, but I could not save her. She was dying. When the paramedics arrived, I sat on the ground motionless and exhausted. I begged them to save my Mother. I watched as they hoisted her heavy frame on to a gurney, strapped her in, and wheeled her into the awaiting ambulance. The wailing sirens cranked on and the lights blinded my vision. As they traveled down the street I listened as the sirens got further and further away until I couldn't hear them anymore. The silence shook me back into reality and I peeled myself off the asphalt parking lot.

I learned that the ambulance had taken my Mother to Midway Hospital. Dr. Maxey assured me that they would do everything humanly possible to save her life. I'm not sure how I got to the hospital. I must have driven myself, but it is a complete blur in my mind. What I do know is that when I arrived at the hospital, I was there, alone. I had tried calling Tommy at his office, but he wasn't there. I didn't have anyone there. My sister was gone and my Mother, my life, my breath was in a hospital bed being poked and prodded and pumped back to life. I needed her to be saved. I wanted her to be saved. In that moment I had never felt so alone. My world was crumbling and I had no one there to help me dig out from under the weight of my fear and ultimate sorrow.

I prayed and cried and sat. That cadence remained for what felt like hours. The doctors and nurses looked like worker ants. They were operating fast and in unison. There was an occasional set of words spoken that I can only guess were orders by the doctors. I watched this dance of doctors and nurses until Dr. Maxey arrived. When he arrived and went into the room to see my Mother and talk with the doctors. I remember seeing him through the small rectangular window of my Mother's room. Almost instantly after he entered the room, the hustle and bustle had stopped and the hurried motions of the hospital staff that existed moments before was over. The fast-moving nurses and doctors had changed their rapid gait to a solemn slog. I didn't know what was happening and I was all alone. When Dr. Maxey emerged from the room, I struggled to stand to my feet. I was weak. We locked eyes in the hall. It felt like an eternity passed before he reached me. His flat affect and empty stare told me what he was about to say before he opened his mouth. The silence of the day is still deafening. I felt her breathe so many times in my ear. I got lost in her hugs and was intoxicated by her kisses. She was more than a Mother, she was my inspiration, my muse, my teacher, and my everything. I couldn't and still can't imagine not having her here. When he reached me, I dropped to my knees, inconsolable. He hadn't said the words. He didn't have to. I knew. In my heart, I knew. Dr. Maxey held me as I wailed in anguish at the loss of my Mother. It was carnal and raw. It physically hurt. My entire body went rigid and numb. Every muscle ached. My legs lost feeling and my head throbbed. My ears rang and the blood that pumped through my body ran cold. I felt my heart break. Dr. Maxey stood me up, then gingerly placed me back in the chair in the waiting room. The room was empty, and so was I. Even though Dr. Maxey was there, I was alone.

I asked Dr. Maxey if I could go into the room where my lifeless Mother's body lay. I wanted to see her before they moved her. They granted me permission to see her. I wanted to see her. Before I entered the room, the doctors had closed her eyes, cleaned her face, and disconnected all the lines that had been utilized to save her life. They didn't. My legs felt as heavy as lead, my head as light as air. I couldn't walk. I stood in the waiting room stiff with grief. I was a stone statue of despair and couldn't move. How could I enter a room where my Mother lay dead? My mind tried to process the moment, but my body had not caught up. It was rigid and limp all at the same time. I felt like my limbs would fall off or that my body would crumble like a demolished building if I took a step. My usual swift walk was reduced to the shuffle of a person who had been paralyzed and just now taking their first attempt at walking again. My body and soul were out of my own control. I wasn't fully there in body or mind. I mean, I was there, but I was having a complete out-of-body experience. Just beyond my dazed gaze, beyond the rectangular framed window, lay my Mother. My mind couldn't comprehend such pain and sadness. I entered that room alone and saw my beloved Mother lying still and peaceful under a crisp white sheet.

I reached down to touch the deep mahogany brown skin of her full cheek and she felt like cold clay. I kissed her and talked to her. I struggled to see if there were any signs of life. There weren't. I imagined that she would awaken with a smile and her hearty laugh. She didn't. I studied her chest to see if it would rise and fall in perfect rhythm. It didn't. I told her that I would take care of Grannie until the end of her days. I told her how much I loved her. I loved my Mother. Some things she did during my life, I didn't understand, but I was and still am grateful for her and all that she has done for me. At that moment, a part of my soul died. I never thought I could live in this world without Burnie and now, how would I live without my Mother?

Later that day, I drove myself to Flagstone to talk to the staff. Flagstone had been our first California home, and I had to share that my Mother, their Big Mama, and the pillar of our family, was gone. I called a few family members and they took the reins and called the others. I was the worker, but this time, I couldn't be anything but sad. I was finally able to reach Tommy and he dropped everything and rushed to McClaney Estate. I slept most of the day. I ordered some personal security to guard me and the house as I had done when Burnie died. I was numb, tired, sad, and lost. My beloved Mother, the source of my earthly joy, was gone. The house was cold. As my grandmother lay in her room, unaware of what was happening, I sat wondering how to tell her that her daughter, her beloved Eula had died. She was in her late 90s and she wept like a baby after hearing the news. No Mother should have to bury their child. I didn't believe that she nor I would ever know joy again. The women in my family have gone through tremendous gain and devastating loss. Once again, a Mother bore the pain of losing a child and I was there, both times, to witness the hurt and pain. In this day and age, mothers, particularly Black Mothers, are losing their children to violence and police brutality and my heart aches for them, just like it ached for my grandmother and my Mother when they lost their children. The Bible says that to be absent from the body is to be present with the Lord. I found only a morsel of comfort in that moment knowing that my Mother was resting in the arms of our Savior.

I have never loved anyone as much as I loved my Mother. There was no one left to step in to take her place. I had to not only continue my role in the family but now, hers too. I mustered some strength and began making all the arrangements for her service. I had to decide which church would be large enough to accommodate the throngs of people that would surely come to pay their respects.

I contacted Dr. William Saxe Epps, the then pastor of Second Baptist Church in Los Angeles to request the use of the church for her services. It was the largest church that I knew of at the time. He and the congregation at Second Baptist welcomed our family with open arms. They were kind and accommodating to us and I am forever in their debt for their generosity and care. The day of my Mother's funeral, I was a shell of myself. I don't remember much because my mind was racing, and my heart was broken. Tommy stood by my side the entire day and didn't leave me once. He steadied my walk and held my hand as I watched person after person pay their respects. With every word spoken, a droplet of love filled my empty cup. I was depleted and drained. Those that spoke, talked about her as a businesswoman and a philanthropist, a real estate mogul and a civic leader. I just wanted them to talk about my Mom.

The family processed in while I watched and waited to see if I had enough energy to follow. My lead legs returned, and Tommy had to physically hold me up as I struggled to take every step. I was walking, but with every step that I took toward the front of the church, I fell further and further away from the reality of the moment. When I finally got to my seat, I exhaled and breathed out the breath that I had hoped would have saved my Mother. It didn't and there she lay. I have never seen so many people in one room. Mayor Tom Bradley and several other dignitaries were in attendance, not out of political duty, simply because they were friends of our family. The service went astonishingly well and to everyone's surprise, I spoke. I have been through a lot in my life, but this was, by far, the hardest thing I have ever had to do. It was God's grace that got me through it. My Mother was the love of my life.

When I came out of the hypnotic stupor of her funeral, I found myself back at Forest Lawn Cemetery in Hollywood Hills this time burying my Mom. Three of the five plots had been filled: Georgia Mae, Burnie, and now my Mother, Eula McClaney. When I arrived home, some dear friends of ours that owned Aunt Kizzy's Back Porch, a soul food restaurant in Marina Del Rey, California, had brought food to feed the masses of people that congregated. The repast was closed to the public and I made it simple for family and close friends to come in, eat, and bask in the glow of my Mother's spirit that hovered over the beautiful grounds that she built on hard work, sacrifice, and sweet potato pies. I will never forget standing on the rear terrace in disbelief that my Mommy was gone. I was approached by a man that I didn't know and was shaken back into the reality of the day. Here stood a foreign man on my terrace. He identified himself as an insurance investigator and wanted to speak with me privately. He told me that he knew my Mom had died of natural causes and that he had also attended the funeral services. He offered me his condolences and wanted me to know that the large insurance policy that was taken out on my Mom would be paid in full. I couldn't believe we were having this conversation and I had just buried my Mom. I ushered him to the front door and security met him there. Insurance money is what he believed was paramount in this moment. Money. Money was never my focus. It was never my Mother's focus. We had wealth, but I would give everything away just to have my Mother back.

As the days and weeks passed after my Mother's death, I stayed home most days and nights with my grandmother. The house was eerily quiet. It was always a peaceful space, but without my Mother, there was an energy that was missing. It was like the walls cried out for her. Nothing was ever the same there. A once robust and lively home full of people and laughter, was reduced to just four walls and a roof. It was a house, not a home. Granny and I spent our time quiet, never discussing the death of my Mother with each other. I think it was just too painful for both of us. I had promised my Mother that I would take good care of my grandmother until the Lord called her home. And He did in 1990. She was 100 years old. Again, I was back at Forest Lawn Cemetery on December 27, 1990, this time, burying my grandmother. My whole family, except for my Father, whom I hadn't seen since Burnie's funeral, was gone. I was alone.

After my grandmother's death, the usual parade of condolences occurred. I had become accustomed to it now. People sent flowers and food, cards, and condolences. Weeks later, the sentiments stopped. People returned to their normal lives and I was by myself in the home that once housed three generations of McClaney/Hendrick women. Cars would drive past the gates and I know people would dream of living in the big white house behind the electric gates. If they knew the pain and sadness that I was experiencing at that time, I imagine that they would run for the hills.

After my Mother's death, I decided that a retreat from all social activities was necessary. I decided to focus on **MY** life and the direction I would now go. I entered yet another new world, but this time, I entered alone. I sent letters to all the organizations that I was involved in. Except for The Links, Incorporated, National Parks and Recreation Association (NRPA), and Delta Sigma Theta Sorority, Incorporated, I resigned all my other memberships. I realized that I was busy being busy and now, I wanted to live my life truly living. I was determined to carry on, I just didn't know how.

In 1988, I closed Flagstone Guest Haven. Since I no longer had a church home, I joined West Angeles Church of God in Christ. It has been a wonderful experience for my life. I needed to find a church home where I could worship and learn more about my Savior Jesus Christ. There, I met my Pastor, Bishop Charles E. Blake, Sr., and his wife, First Lady Mae L. Blake. I was at the lowest point in my life soon after my Mother's death and they stepped in and held me up. I believe that they were sent into my life by God, with a little help from my Mother and Burnie. West Angeles became my second home, a church home where I felt comfortable and where the uncompromised Word of God was taught. I dove headfirst into the church. I co-chaired an event to benefit Save Africa's Children along with Bishop Blake. Save Africa's Children was an organization founded by Bishop and First Lady Blake after they returned from a trip they took to Africa. They saw the conditions of the children and were compelled to do more than just talk about their experiences. For 10 years, I served side-by-side with Bishop Blake to raise hundreds of thousands of dollars for the children of Africa. I even took trips to several African countries to see our work at work. Visiting the Motherland was transformative. In the faces of the children I saw hope and possibility. They were the faces of me and Burnie and all those friends that played in the play yard in Pittsburgh. I went to Ghana, Zimbabwe, Cape Town, Johannesburg, and other places in Africa. My greatest experience was when I visited Robben Island where Nelson Mandela was incarcerated for 27 years. It was a life-changing experience for me to walk into his cell and lay down on the floor where he had been until he was liberated and later became President of South Africa. I also had the privilege of meeting Bishop Desmond Tutu on that trip.

And then, I walked through the twisted corridors of Elmina Castle. Elmina Castle was erected by the Portuguese in 1482 as Castelo de São Jorge da Mina, also known as Castelo da Mina or simply Mina, in present-day Elmina, Ghana. This sacred space was the first trading post built on the Gulf of Guinea, and the oldest European building in existence south of the Sahara. First established as a trade settlement, the castle later became one of the most important stops on the route of the Transatlantic Slave Trade. In 1637, the Dutch seized the fort from the Portuguese after an unsuccessful attempt to do so in 1596. The Dutch subsequently took over the Portuguese Gold Coast in 1642. The slave trade from Elmina Castle continued under Dutch rule until 1814. In 1872, the Dutch Gold Coast, including the fort, became a possession of Great Britain. As awful as its seeds are, what sprang forth from Elmina Castle is a forest of beauty, unbelievable history, and the triumph of a people that should not have, by all accounts, survived. The walls hold our history and the sound of the souls of my ancestors. Walking through the corridors, I felt the roughness of the walls and soaked in the breath of my people. Over one doorway, rests an unassuming sign that reads, *The Door of No Return*. It was the last door that captive Africans went through before they were savagely transported from their African roots to foreign lands where they would be raped, beaten, and worked to death. If they survived the Middle Passage, they would be hauled in groups to an auction block and sold like hogs to the highest bidder. I felt the souls of my ancestors in the corridors of Elmina Castle and inhaled their sorrow as I walked through the door of no return. I said a silent prayer of gratitude to them. I committed that day to live life to the fullest, because they had been denied the choice. I had experienced tremendous loss, but my ancestors survived loss in ways that I could never imagine, and they fought to live, not only for themselves, but for the generations of descendant to come. Because of them, I am, and I owe it to them to live a full life dedicated to service.

I rediscovered myself in Africa. Everywhere I went, I saw my people. It was beautiful. They were beautiful. I felt at home for the first time in a long time. I saw the faces of the women and in them, I saw my Mother and sister. Many of the vendors at the marketplace were women. I learned that there were significantly fewer men because of the AIDS epidemic and war. These women were often single and singlehandedly making a living for themselves and their children. I admired them for that. They were busy making things and selling them to eager buyers. They were creating their own empires with simple materials and pocketing the money as they went. I loved that. It was inspirational. While marveling at the beauty of the products being sold in one of the open markets, I asked a woman selling her wares to help me find 100 children as quickly as she could. At first, she looked at me with a side eye. I told her that I was an American businesswoman and I wanted to buy 100 children gifts. She smiled and agreed to gather the children. Before I knew what was happening, children were coming from every corner of the market! Children came from everywhere. Hundreds of children all with their bright, beautiful faces surrounded me. There was hopeful anticipation in their smiles and they began to dance with delight at the mere prospect of what was to come. I proceeded to take 100 children shopping for clothing and shoes. The woman who helped gather the children watched with glee as I managed to get all the children outfitted. In their faces I saw the legacy of my family. They were my people, my children. My Mother had given birth to this family legacy, and I was charged to continue it in those children. When I returned to my hotel room after hours of shopping, I was exhausted. Physically, I felt fine, but I was emotionally drained. My heart was full, and my soul sang, but my emotions were all over the place. I knew that my love for children was going to be revisited at some point, I just didn't know when or how. Until God showed me, I rested in the knowledge that for one small moment, I changed the lives of 100 children in Africa, and they changed an American businesswoman's life forever.

My African adventure continued, and I visited schools and hospitals and participated in church activities. Going to the Continent of Africa is an experience every human on earth should have. We all originate there and going back is like a homecoming of sorts. You connect with the people, the soil, and the energy. Being there took me back to those years when life was simple and there was so much hope and promise. There is beauty in building. I loved those years of unpredictability and want. It was in those times that we were the most creative and bold. We mastered the business as a family. We gave ourselves permission to fail and succeed. Africa, my Motherland, gave that to me. She reminded me of the strong and creative blood that runs through my veins. Africa showed me that even though we struggled then, what was most important was the relationship that we have to our roots and to our family. In those early years, our family was complete and intact, and I had spent way too much time longing for those days. When I allowed myself to let go of the past and push forward, I was able to take the family legacy to an entirely new level. Sometimes, you feel stuck in your life. I did. I made a decision that I was no longer going to live like that. I realized that sometimes you must look back in order to correct your errors, but more often than not, those errors are uncorrectable. In the event that that is the case, then your only way to stay sane and focused is to speak the issue and then move on. Because I didn't have a dog in the fight of my parents' marriage, I didn't have a stake in how to make it better in my mind. I had to accept that it just didn't work out and that is fine. With this newfound revelation, I returned home and focused my attention on maintaining the remaining properties in our real estate portfolio. I also extended my reach to serve as many people as humanly possible.

Changing my Path

I had been asked to join several boards during this season in my life. Sitting on a corporate board can be a daunting task. There are meetings, fundraisers, and management of the structure of the business or organization. When the request came for board membership for the National Parks and Recreation Association (NRPA), I was flattered, and gob smacked. During my tenure as a member of the Board of Directors of the NRPA, I was fortunate to serve the community in a brand-new way. I traveled to Alaska on one of our many excursions. Alaska was beautiful. It truly is the Last Frontier. True to my roots, I also began to host parties again. During our annual meeting that was held in Santa Barbara, I arranged to transport the entire Board to my home. They boarded luxury buses that carried them from Santa Barbara to Holmby Hills. When they arrived, I threw a magnificent party at McClaney Estate. A team of synchronized swimmers performed as we sat poolside for dinner. I also hired several celebrity impersonators to mesmerize the crowd. It was a grand affair. I treated the Board to champagne and caviar as a send-off from the party. I have always loved a good party, but after my Mother's death, I thought my life was over and that I would never be able to throw parties or have fun again. I decided that I had a choice to make — live or die. To live meant that I needed to accept my reality and grow further into service to the world. To die meant that I would waste my life wallowing in self-pity and despair. I decided to live.

I established a home office where I could conduct the business of McClaney Properties. It was a quiet and serene place for me to work and create a new legacy for our family. Though I was safe, I also felt isolated because my estate sits behind tall electric gates. I spent every day in my office working from 4:00 AM to 5:00 PM. I think those years were spent building upon my Mother's legacy and creating a distraction from the reality of my losses. My friends and relatives understood my stance and gave me the space I needed. After much consideration, I started selling a few properties. I maintained enough of the portfolio to keep myself active and engaged.

A few years later, I was invited to Las Vegas, Nevada to visit my cousin's church. He and his family had moved there from Los Angeles a year before my visit. Pastor Clinton House and his wife, Dr. Mary House were assigned to a church there. They invited me to speak to their congregation about my Mother's newly published book, *God, I Listened*. She began writing her memoirs shortly after Burnie died. Her story was compelling and needed to be told. Pastor House was intrigued by her book, so I accepted the invitation to speak. I prepared for days for this opportunity. My objective was to move the crowd in such a way that they would be able to find strength through my Mother's struggles. I put on my Sunday best and readied myself to speak publicly about my Mother for the first time since her funeral. To my surprise, when I arrived to speak, 26 eyes were staring back at me. Thirteen people where in the church. Here I was telling an intimate story about my successful Mother and there were only 13 people there to hear me, and most of them were children. I was undeterred and spoke about my Mother to the 13 parishioners as though there were 1,000.

After the church gathering, I left feeling accomplished. I laughed to myself because my Mother would have gotten a kick out of just 13 people sitting in the audience. She would have seen those 26 eyes staring back at her and she would have stopped her speech, tossed some chicken in seasoned flour, and fried it in a vat of clean grease and prepared a plate for each of them. I wasn't my Mother and instead of frying chicken, I asked my cousin to have a broker show me some properties in the Las Vegas area. My cousins were living in a small two-bedroom apartment with two small children and a dog. I quickly found a house, purchased it, and made arrangements for them to live in it rent-free for four years. My desire was for Pastor House to spend his time learning and preaching the Word of God. I didn't want him to have to worry about paying rent or a mortgage. They were good stewards and have since built a magnificent church. Their congregation of 13 has grown to over 4,500 parishioners. Between his preaching power and her singing voice, Pastor and First Lady House are changing hearts and minds in Sin City. Mountaintop Faith Ministries is a beacon of light and love in the Las Vegas community. Dr. Mary House has a singing voice that can captivate an entire church body. Not only does she sing, she has a warm spirit that emanates the love of God.

I had learned the landscape of Las Vegas and I decided to venture into the real estate market there. I bought many houses and rented them out. The crown jewel of my Vegas properties was a large beautiful two-story house with six bedrooms and seven bathrooms in the exclusive area of Section 10. When I first saw the house, it was exquisite, and I wanted it. The outside was crystal white, and the iron gates were a beautiful geometric design. My broker met me at the property and explained that Section 10 was a highly sought-after area of Las Vegas. We approached the front door and were met by the current owners, a Greek family with three teenage children. They were pleasant enough, so we made small talk. They kept saying that they believed that my husband and children would be happy in this area. They assumed that I was married with several children. Why else would a single woman look at such a large home to purchase? I laughed as I thought about their bias. At least they didn't judge me because I am Black. Their bias came in the form of believing that a single Black woman couldn't be in a financial position to buy a home of that size and price by herself. My Mother had done so years before and I was determined to do so as well. The first floor had a living room, a formal dining room, den, office, bedroom, laundry room, two bathrooms, and a large kitchen. Upstairs were five bedrooms all en suite. I shopped for furniture in Los Angeles and Las Vegas to fill up this 6,000-square-foot house. I wanted to have a home in Las Vegas when I visited that would have the same elegance as the McClaney Estate in Holmby Hills.

I purchased homes in Las Vegas and opened them as foster care facilities. I had always had a heart for foster children since our days in Pittsburgh, so I founded JEB Enterprises, named after my Grandmother, Joanna, my Mother, Eula, and my sister, Burnie. JEB was a non-profit organization dedicated to the establishment and management of foster care homes. I loved the children and I enjoyed every moment of time I spent with them. The social workers would clamor for placement in my homes. The houses had beauty, an exceptional location, and a wonderful reputation. Our homes rarely had a vacancy. Because I was concerned that only White children were being placed in my homes, I questioned the social worker and asked why there were no Black children being placed. She gave me a canned answer, "Dr. McClaney, there is no intentional mistake. We chose the children at random." I knew different because I had experienced covert racism and palpable microaggressions all of my life, so I certainly was not going to let some social worker dictate who was placed in my homes. Sadly, social services had other ideas. I signed the anti-discrimination policy and therefore, had to accommodate all children. I complied with the law and licensing board regulations, but I was still bothered.

During the summertime, as a vacation for my staff, I would have them bring all the children to McClaney Estate in Holmby Hills for two weeks. Their visit was like sleep away camp on steroids. I made sure that each child had personalized pajamas and I bought tons of toys, crafts, and games. We traveled to the beach and to the mountains. They loved frolicking through the house, and they enjoyed swimming in my nearly Olympic sized pool that is situated at the front of house, just below the elevated porch. They played hide-and-seek in the same gardens where celebrities had taken engagement pictures and where our legendary parties took place. They roller skated on the same driveway where 1,000 people once listened to Pastor Chuck Singleton preach his sermon at the first Gospel Songfest, which he continued for 27 years. They played checkers sitting on the terrace where I wept so deeply when my Mother died. Their presence changed the energy of my home. No longer did I see spaces and places as vessels of sad memories. Those same places were filled with childhood laughter and pure unmarred joy. The experience was extremely rewarding and cathartic. Those five years were some of the best years of my life. I dissolved JEB Enterprises in the late 1990s. I wanted to relax and not be responsible for attending parent-teacher conferences, enduring evaluations with social workers, and preparing monthly reports. The Department of Social Services hated to see me go, but it was time for me to move on. I think of my children often and pray that I was able to provide them a little joy in their lives. They certainly gave me boatloads in mine.

I began having large, lavish parties at the Las Vegas home which, I named McClaney Estate Las Vegas. The house was made to host parties. It was grand and the grounds were breathtaking. I gave a large outdoor all-white party well before Diddy ever thought to do it. The Crystal Ball was a party for no reason at all. Guests came from California, New York, Las Vegas, Georgia, and Russia. All the guests wore white and naturally, I arrived at the party in a black designer gown from Paris, France.

I also hosted a party for the NRPA Board in Las Vegas. I decided on a Western theme and I named my home The McClaney Ponderosa for that party. Everyone wore Western inspired outfits and were given cowboy hats at the door. Staff members from the Las Vegas Parks and Recreation Department provided luxury buses that would bring the board members to and from their hotel. The buses ran every 30 minutes until the conclusion of the event. We feasted on barbecue ribs, pork, beef, chicken, and all the trimmings. In another section of the backyard, I had a professional dancer teaching my guests how to do western line dancing. My parties in Las Vegas were wonderful, just as they were in Holmby Hills and at the Lewis Estate in Pittsburgh.

I spent a great deal of my time celebrating in those days. I'm not sure if I was escaping the sense of loss, distracting myself from the work that had consumed so much of my life, or a combination of all of those things, but that season awakened a new part of me. Burnie was the social butterfly and she had hundreds of friends. She was able to create relationships with people from every walk of life. I have always been semi-social, but my parties became more lavish and attended by more people because I was coming into my own way of doing and being. That season was liberating and though I missed my sister and Mother, I felt their spirits guiding me to embody all that they had been. I created the most beautiful spaces in our home and decided that it would be a place of celebration, rather than sorrow. The parties at the Las Vegas Estate were the talk of the town, but my Christmas parties in Holmby Hills were the most sought-after invitation amongst the community in Los Angeles, Beverly Hills, Bel Air, and, of course, Holmby Hills. I spared no expense and the guestlist read like a who's who of politicians, celebrities, executives, and the founders of some of most successful American brands in the world.

On September 11, 2001, the world changed forever. The terrorist attacks on the World Trade Center, the Pentagon, and Flight 93 killed 2,974 people. Like most Americans, I know exactly where I was that fateful day. I arose at 4:00 AM like always. I was preparing to go to my office in Century City when a news flash appeared on *Good Morning America* that a plane had hit the World Trade Center in New York City. Moments later, another tower was hit. Then the Pentagon. Then flight 93 went missing. I thought that the world was coming to an end that day. I watched as the Twin Towers collapsed into a pile of rubble. We all sat in stunned terror as people hurled themselves from the buildings to their death. I had been in those towers for meetings and dinners on several occasions, and I always marveled at the sheer majesty of their size and beauty. I could hardly imagine what was happening right before my very eyes. It was a devastating day. For days and weeks following the attacks, the news reports were on a constant loop discussing the death, destruction, and panic that our country was in that day. I was at a loss. I wasn't fearful, because I knew God was ultimately in control of it all, but I was afraid for those who didn't know Him, and His grace and I wept thinking about the families of those that were missing and whose bodies were, subsequently never recovered. I recalled praying extensively for them. More than anything, however, I wanted to do something that would have a lasting impact. I prayed and the Lord told me to dedicate that year's Christmas party to the victims of 9/11, their families, and the brave first responders that sacrificed their own lives in an effort to save so many more. Initially, I thought it was a crazy idea – having a party that highlighted the events of 9/11, but the more I began to plan it, it became crystal clear that it was exactly what my 2001 Christmas party was to be about.

I hired the best event planners, event designers, and florists to transform my home into an Americana themed winter wonderland. I purchased 50 flocked Christmas trees that were strategically placed in all the windows, on the grounds, on the veranda, and in the interior of the house. Each tree was decorated with hundreds of red, white, and blue handmade ornaments. I requested that all the guests wear red, white, or blue to the event. I hired traditional Dickens carolers to serenade my guests as they walked the grounds toward the house. Donned in velvet dresses, fur muffs, and morning coats, the singers sang traditional Christmas songs to the delight of the partygoers. The feeling was warm and wonderful. Every person in attendance had witnessed the devastation of that unforgettable September day and had known someone or been associated with someone that perished or that had narrowly escaped death. I wanted to transport my guests back into a simpler time in history as they crisscrossed the grounds. Then, I had the carolers guide them into the house where the décor was overwhelmingly patriotic. I wanted the house to reflect the emotion and pride that we all felt in those days after the attack. The Nation was grieving, and we needed each other to get through this horrific time. As the guests entered, you could feel the collective sigh of relief. There were hugs and tears all around. People had been holding their breath in those weeks and months after, and we were all gauging each other to determine when, or if, we could enjoy life again.

I can imagine Lorne Micheals experienced the same trepidation when he decided to air *Saturday Night Live* only 18 days after the attack. We didn't know if we were allowed to laugh and smile after the loss of so many American citizens. That party was just what we all needed, and I made sure that all 250 guests left with an ornament and the promise that they would be welcomed back the following year.

What was most important to me that night, was that the party was an escape for the collective reality that we were all facing. People on television were lamenting about travel changes and restrictions, and all I could think about was how the loved ones of the 2,974 people lost would manage the holidays without their family members. I knew what they were feeling. The "first" or all things after a tragedy is never easy. Birthdays. Christmas. Thanksgiving. Those families had to endure them all right after their world turned upside down. I felt their pain and knew all too well the depth of despair that they experienced. During the evening, I quieted the guests and offered a prayer for the country. I recall the sheer weight of the moment. I looked around the room and saw every race, socioeconomic standing, and religion represented. Here we were, in a home designed by a Black man who was unable to sit on the same side of a table as his White clients, that was now owned by a woman whose mother started their empire selling sweet potato pies, praying in the foyer for a Nation that was attacked by terrorists. No Hollywood writers could create such a story. I spoke on how grateful I was that God saw fit to bring us all together to pray and honor the lives of those 2,974 souls. I encouraged everyone in that room to use whatever influence they had to help our neighbors and countrymen. "We must be the change we want to see in the world," I said. "We are responsible for what happens next and to never forget the past so that we never repeat it in our future." I quoted my good friend, and world-renowned motivational speaker, Les Brown, "As long as you can look up, you can get up no matter what your situation is." We had to decide how we wanted to navigate after such tragedy. I, for one, was changed forever and made the commitment to get up, look up, and be the change I wanted to see in the world. Everyone in that room owed a debt of gratitude to those who made sure we, as a Nation, were safe and secure, but we also needed to ensure that the next generation was better than the prior. I, along with several others, committed to give more freely and serve more faithfully in the world. I also committed to open my home more readily to people and organizations that desired to create a more perfect Union. This was to be a house of healing, restoration, and celebration. It was at that party that turned my home into the place where hope lives and change begins. I am solicited weekly for the use of my home for films, weddings, receptions, or other events. I am very selective about the energy that flows in and out of it. It has always been a sacred space, but after that party in December 2001, I became more conscientious and determined to celebrate the good in the world and find ways to solve the bad.

All my Christmas parties are legendary. Whether they occur after a national tragedy, or themed to suit a particular style, they have always been a highlight for my guests. I recall one year I requested that all the women wear red. I made a trip to Neiman Marcus on Wilshire Boulevard to shop for a green gown to wear. It is a practice of mine to ask my guests to wear a particular color to my parties, just for me to show up in a completely different color. When I was met by my concierge for the day at Neiman's, she asked if I was there to purchase a red dress. I laughed because she said that a hundred women had been to the store in the past few weeks, all clamoring to find the perfect red dress to wear at, what they characterized as, the party of the season. She asked me if I was attending the party and I told her, "No…I'm hosting it." She then thanked me because with all the red dresses that were purchased, her commission was going to be HUGE. That party singlehandedly paid for a well-deserved vacation for my Neiman Marcus concierge.

For every event, I make sure that my guests have a full and complete experience. Most parties I attend are beautifully decorated, well-attended, and have exquisite cuisine, but I desire for my guests to have all of that and be fully immersed in whatever theme I have created. From the invitation to the moment their car is retrieved by the valet attendants, I want them to feel special and as though their presence was necessary for the party to be complete. I want them to feel the way my Mother felt that day that she received her honorary doctorate – important and worthy of excellence. From the valets that park their cars, to the wait staff that serve the cuisine, to the design of the tablescapes, the themes that I have created are carried out fully. I have had a Santa themed party where the staff wore his signature hat, an all-white Christmas party where the ballroom was draped in floor-to-ceiling silk and the waitstaff wore white tuxedos with tails. I created a winter wonderland complete with polar bears and snow on the grounds, and even hired children to frolic and build snowmen. I hire the best florist in Los Angeles to create extraordinary arrangements and the best caterers to feed my guests. I have even been known to change the interior furnishings of my home to fit the theme. My Mother's furniture from Gilbert's Fine Furniture has been reupholstered several times and has stood the test of time, even when I've transformed it to fit a particular party theme.

My love for events often marries with my love of people and important causes that I believe in. This marriage creates a beautiful synergy between what I can provide and what the public servant can do for the greater good and the community at-large. I can say that several Black politicians, that have run for public office in Southern California since 1975, have had an event at McClaney Estate. If your politics are not built on truth and compassion for our fellow man, for example, you will not be able to have an event at my home.

It may seem silly and frivolous to spend money on parties, but those parties are more than food, drinks, and music. They are a means for people from all stations in life to come together, with one common goal, to celebrate. In my teen years when my parents threw those cocktail parties, many relationships, business deals, and political decisions were made. I believe that the same is true for the events that I host now. In the recent years, I came to the decision that I would no longer have parties that were inconsequential. I have become intentional about everything I do. Whether it is writing a book, hosting an event, or developing relationships, *why* I do *what* I do is more important to me than *what* I do. I suppose I have taken that trait from my Mother. There were many times that I didn't understand the *why*. I have learned that you must set your intentions before you begin anything. Know your *why* so that your *why* will guide your *what*.

My affinity for social activity extends far beyond parties and events at my home. I am a frequent guest at The Polo Lounge located inside the Beverly Hills Hotel. In early 1911, Margaret J. Anderson, a wealthy widow, and her son, Stanley S. Anderson, who had been managing the Hollywood Hotel, ordered the construction of the Beverly Hills Hotel, near Burton Green's mansion. Burton Green was an oil tycoon and real estate developer who had purchased land in the foothills of the Santa Monica Mountains. He began building mansions on the land, including his own residence, investing $500,000. Because of the hefty price tag, he had difficulty selling the other property. He hired the Anderson's to build a hotel, which he named *Beverly Farms*, after his home in Massachusetts, believing that it would attract people to the area, billing it as "halfway between Los Angeles and the sea". The May 11, 1911, edition of the *Los Angeles Times* announced the news that a "huge Mission-style hotel" was to be built by Anderson, with the motto that "her guests were entitled to the best of everything regardless of cost." What sprang up from the ground was a pink building that stood as a beacon of wealth and posh living in the middle of a still developing Beverly Hills community.

In the 1930s, The Beverly Hills Hotel was purchased by Hernando Courtright. Courtright was a native of Coeur d'Alene, Idaho who spent most of his childhood in San Francisco. In 1941, Courtright, was the vice president of the Bank of America. He, along with friends Irene Dunne, Loretta Young, and Harry Warner, purchased the hotel. The Beverly Hills Hotel boasts 210 rooms and suites, 23 bungalows, and the trademark pink and green exterior. This purchase was his first venture into the hotel business. During his tenure, he took a bold step by enlisting the services of famed Black architect Paul Williams, (yes, the same architect that build my home) to construct the Crescent Wing of the hotel, what by then was affectionately known as the "Pink Palace" because of its exterior color. Courtright created the Polo Lounge after a discussion with his friend, Charles Wrightsman, who led a national championship polo team. Wrightsman felt it improper to keep the team trophy, a silver bowl, in his own home. Courtright, upon hearing his friend's predicament, offered to display the bowl in the hotel's bar, which was being redecorated at the time. The name for the bar and its lounge sprang from that favor. Thus, The Polo Lounge was born.

I love the restaurant for another reason. I am not particularly fond of polo, but the interior of The Polo Lounge, with its forest green walls and white crown molding and baseboards reminds me of Lewis Estate. Every time I enter that space I am transported back into a beautiful time in my life. Friends that I have lunched with there don't know why it is always my first choice to dine. But the fact is, I love it there. I walk into the foyer and I envision me and my Dad painting those walls. The green hue is exactly the same color that was splattered on my overalls as we painstakingly dragged brushes to paint. The crystal white molding is as white as snow. I only wish that one day, I could look out and see pink plastic flamingos strategically placed across the hotel grounds! The Polo Lounge staff has always been so gracious to me. They know me by name, and I know them as well.

I also enjoy dining at The Ivy. Many people know The Ivy as a celebrity hot spot or where you go to people watch. I, on the other hand enjoy The Ivy because of its simple organic beauty. When I go, I always sit outside among the gardens and greenery that surround the tables. The grounds look like a Bermuda Shorts Party could break out at any moment. The flowers and trees take me back to my teen years in Pittsburgh.

Friend and Foe

I have always had malcontents (haters!) in my life. Every so often they bubble to the surface of my life trying to break me. Let me be very clear, I have been bent many times, but I have never been broken. There will **ALWAYS** be haters in life. It is an unfortunate truth, but it is my truth, and if you have any measure of success, it will be your truth too. I think anyone who has had any measure of success has people who do not wish them well. No matter how much I have given, there will always be people in my life that do not want me happy, healthy, or wealthy. I am fully aware, even now, that some of those that read this book are only doing so to celebrate my failures and mistakes. Thankfully, both have been steppingstones in my life, and I count all my life experiences as opportunities for growth and development. I suppose if you have gotten to this point of my memoirs, you have discovered that there is not much that holds me back. Haters have not, and they never will. I want to share what I have learned in my life about how to deal with them.

Let me begin by saying that I know thousands of people. I am fully aware that everyone I know and that knows me, is not my friend. I keep a very close circle and if I consider you a friend, you know that you are without reservation. I have always been very selective about my relationships. From my days collecting rents, to those lean years at Flagstone, my relationships have always been cultivated over time and very important to me. I have, however, dealt with my share of haters in my day. I have been stolen from, taken advantage of, allowed people to live in my home rent free, given away money, purchased flights, cars, and clothes for people who would turn around and stab me in the back, speak ill of me, and try to destroy my reputation. God has given me the ability to see the intention of people before their actions manifest. I have endured unbelievable hurt at the hands of those who I have confided in and trusted. My response remains consistent. I do not seek revenge or wish harm on anyone who has hurt me. Rather, I bid them farewell out of my life, pray for God to have mercy on them for their misgivings, and move on. It is of no benefit to me to retaliate or seek revenge. In fact, I do the direct opposite when I am betrayed. I pray for those that have treated me poorly. It is important to remember that God is in control of everything, even the things that hurt. I step aside and let Him work out those situations.

Instead of discussing specific incidents, I offer to you the lessons that I have learned about dealing with the haters in your life. This would be a good time to get a highlighter or an ink pen, you are about to go to school!

1. Become more aware of what is REALLY worth your energy.

2. Misery often loves company.

3. If you find yourself gossiping about others, just know that others are gossiping about you.

4. People have a lot to say about lives they have never lived.

5. God reduces your circle because He heard conversations that you didn't.

6. Aspire not to have more, but to be more.

7. Keep your friends close and your enemies OUT OF YOUR LIFE!

8. What you allow is what will continue.

9. Only give up if it doesn't give back.

10. Love your enemies. Let them bring out the best in you, not the worst.

11. Don't worry about the haters…they are just angry because the truth you speak contradicts the lie they live.

12. There is a message in the way that a person treats you, just listen.

13. An apology without change is just manipulation.

14. Expectation is premeditated resentment.

15. Stop expecting **YOU** from other people.

16. Some people only talk about you because they have lost the privileged to talk to you.

Now, take it from me, these lessons are difficult to put into practice every day. But I assure you, if you do, you will find a greater sense of peace and prosperity of soul in your life. I take care of me first! There is no human more important to me than me. If I allowed every cross word, hateful action, or downright nasty behavior to affect me, I would not be able to have joy and serve as I do. If you take nothing else from my memoirs, take this; Your Light and Life ought never be dimmed by those who wish to snuff you out.

The most effective way to ensure your complete healing from hate is to forgive and forget. It has always been my nature to forgive and forget. I learned that lesson from my parents. Their relationship, from my perspective, was typical of marriage in those days. They had their disagreements, but I do not remember them ever being volatile toward each other. I do know that forgiveness was a huge factor in their marriage. I was consistently the mediator in our family. I was always seeking harmony among my parents. I wanted them to be able to communicate and be loving toward each other all the time. Chalk it up to my naivete when I was a child and teen, but I believe that I have the same feelings as an adult. I wanted to forgive my father for how he divorced my mother. I wanted to forgive him for how he left us. I wanted to be my Mother's friend and her daughter. I wanted to forgive myself for having resentment toward my parents for not working out their relationship. I needed to learn to forgive, and finally, I did. I think the tragedy of my parent's divorce bore in me a need to forgive and forget when I have been wronged. I truly believe that forgiveness is giving up the hope that the past could have been any different and forgetting is letting go of the energy it takes to hold on to the past hurts. I forgive and forget everyone who has wronged me. It is really okay! Every single one of those relationships has caused me to be at this beautiful point in my life. For that, I thank my haters for giving me the strength to carry on and serve the world boldly and fearlessly.

Linked for Life

Before the death of my Mother, I made the decision to become more involved in organizations that provided community service and allowed me to have comradery with other professional women. I hadn't been a "girlie girl" as a child and it wasn't my intention to become one as an adult. I did, however, learn the value of having women who were likeminded in my life. I had always known about the Links, Incorporated. Although my Mother was never a member, and in fact, she wasn't the type to belong to a women's organization, she was well-versed on the service that the Links provided. Burnie had made her debut with the Links in Pittsburgh and my Mother was heavily courted to join the membership. She would often say that she had, "no need to lunch with a bunch of women." I understood her position, but in 1980, I joined an interest group in Beverly Hills to start, what would be come, the Beverly Hills West Chapter of the Links, Incorporated. My mother respected my choice and gave her hearty blessing to begin this quest.

In 1946, the Links, Incorporated was founded in Philadelphia when two young Black women, Margaret Hawkins and Sarah Scott, invited seven friends to join them in forming a new type of club. These founders envisioned the Links, Incorporated as an organization that would fill gaps among existing groups by addressing the needs and goals of Black women. They also intended for the organization to serve as a forum for personal friendships and community service. Soon after the Philadelphia group organized, the members began contacting women in other cities who might be interested in establishing similar groups, and by 1949, 10 chapters had been established.

Women, particularly Black women, in those days, were not well regarded in society. The social and political landscape was difficult and harsh for women. At the time that these bold women decided to create this organization, the United States was just emerging from the Great Depression. Harry S. Truman was the President of the United States, and there were major shortages in jobs and housing for those returning from war. For Blacks, the picture was even more grim. Black people were experiencing the height of the Jim Crow era and lynching of our people was at an all-time high. Renowned actor/singer Paul Robeson founded the American Crusade Against Lynching because the atrocity was so out of control. Even during all of that, these courageous women had the sense of mind to serve the greater good by starting this beautiful organization. It was an extraordinary feat that reminds me of the tenacity that my Mother must have had. None of these women allowed their gender, their race, or society to limit their ability to succeed. This legacy continues in the hearts and minds of all members today.

The Links, Incorporated organization has supported civil rights organizations, women's right initiatives, and international human rights efforts. The organization's focus expanded over time. In 1958, the Links added services for youth as a major component of its mission. The organization also added programs addressing educational and health needs in the African Diaspora, and it has sought to address health disparities in the Black community, creating bone-marrow and organ-donor projects and holding events to promote health and wellness. The Links have also worked to increase appreciation for the arts and recognition of Black artists.

I, along with chapter organizer Joyce Black, Shirlee Ellis Amos, Mattie Dobbs, Patricia Gibson, Jamesina E. Henderson, Alexis Camille Jackson, Rosina V. Jackson, Consuelo B. Marshall, Claudette Robinson, Margaret Patricia Rodgers, Jan Rooks, Erleen Scott, Mercedes H. Williams, Sonja L. Thompson, Myrlie Evers Williams, Doris R. Valdry, Pamelia L. Wiltz, Frances Williams, Geraldine P. Woods, Gail E. Wyatt, Mignon M. Wyatt were our charter members. We cemented our position in the National organization, when we became an official chapter on May 25, 1985, thus beginning a yet another new chapter in my life of service and philanthropy.

This group of women hold a dear place in my heart. I have held every Chapter position, with the exception of Financial Secretary. I have held National positions, and most significantly, was appointed Chair of the 1946 Society which consists of members who have donated over $25,000 to the organization. My greatest joy in the organization, however, has been watching the membership grow. I am the only active charter member of the Beverly Hills West Chapter and I am inspired when I see new members enter our beautiful fold, ready willing to take our mission of friendship and service to new heights. These women have held me up and allowed me the freedom to serve in a great capacity and I am ever grateful for that. We have supported each other through marriages and divorces, births and deaths, health and sickness, triumphs, and defeats. What we have always maintained, however, is the collective desire to give of ourselves to make sure others needs are met. The Links have been a staple in my life, and I am grateful that made that step toward membership over 36 years ago.

We are now a thriving chapter who has managed to raise millions of dollars for causes that we support. We have honored dignitaries and ordinary people who have done extraordinary things. We have sponsored countless events and even sent several children to college on scholarship. Our commitment is to the tenets set forth by our National office and to support the community with every financial, physical, and spiritual gift that we have.

Daddy's Girl

My father wasn't a saint. I didn't hate him after the letter, but I did resent him for many years. He was a hurt person who hurt others with his actions. His hatred of my Mother's success and ambitions ultimately ruined our relationship. The relationship that fathers and daughters have with one another is sacred. Ours was no different. After that crucial day when my Mother received that certified letter, I knew my life was never going to be the same with my Father. I had never had any resentment toward him, although, after seeing my Mother's sadness over the years and reading her memoirs, I learned about their marriage in a way that I never knew. I can't say that my view of my Father changed in any particular way, but I can say that reading those words was painful.

Watching my Father paint was like watching ballet. He created art with a paintbrush with a sixth-grade education. His attention to detail and skill is still unmatched. I've hired professional painters to come into my home to paint the exterior and the interior and none have been as gifted as my Dad. His hands were steady and methodical with each stroke of his paint brush. One stroke more perfect than the one prior. I studied him and watched what he did. He patiently taught me everything he knew. I often wonder how he must have felt to be able to teach me something that he knew so well. He never beamed with pride or took credit for my skill. He allowed me to flourish on my own. I believe that is the greatest gift any parent can give a child — the ability for them to succeed on their own. My Father gave that to me in the most beautiful and simple way as we worked side-by-side. We would change surfaces all over our home and at the other properties. Those first few years when he would have me painting radiators, I would emerge from my duties covered in paint. He, on the other hand, wouldn't have a speck on him. He was able to paint with such efficiency. Perhaps it was because his father would have reprimanded him had he splashed one drop of paint on his clothing. I wonder whether or not that was true for my Dad. I wonder if that's the reason he never wanted more because to him more meant more work and more pain. All my Dad ever wanted was peace. He wanted a normal, easy, peaceful life. I'm growing into that type of person now, where easy and peaceful are the staples of my existence. All I want now, after working so hard for so long, is to live a simple, beautiful, peaceful life.

I am truly the product of both of my parents. The first half of my life I was driven and ambitious like my Mother, focused on building this empire, a go-getter in every sense of the word. Now, in this second part of my life I'm very much like my Father, quiet and easy going, no longer striving to gain or build. I am so grateful that they were my parents and that I was able to get the very best parts of them. My only desire is to share with the world all that I know and all that I have learned so that they can then discover the very best parts of them too.

When I was a little girl, I thought my Dad could do things that no one else could do. My Dad could take a bucket of paint and a brush and create the most beautiful spaces. He was able to move the brush along the lines and curves of a wall or door in such a way that he never had to tape anything. I used to watch as the brush strokes would go up and down, side to side, as he painted a radiator, or a house, or a wall. I marveled at how every stroke offered full coverage, never leaving any blank spaces. He was as close to perfect as any human could be in my eyes. He was my everything. I was a daddy's girl, but make no mistake, my Mother was the beat in my heart. Dad was my first love. He was tall, dark, and strong. I see why my Mother thought he was so attractive. I never knew a day where he wasn't working and trying to provide the basics for our family. As he was trying to create a simpler life than what he had left in Alabama, my Mother was striving to build a legacy that surpassed his understanding. My Father was passive compared to my Mother. He wasn't weak, but passive. I think he had to be that way because of the life he had led as the son of his father. My grandfather's hardness ultimately hardened my Father and caused him to be the shell of the man that he could have been. My 83-year-old mind can process all of these things now, but as a child and a teenager I had no idea the depth and breadth of my Father's pain.

When I was a teenager, I never really talked to my Dad about boys. He made very little conversation as related to such subjects. He was, however, adamant that I maintain my chastity until marriage. He knew how boys thought and their desires for young women, like myself and Burnie. I honored him for that, but I often wondered why he was so strict about those things and not about others. What I know for certain is that my Father loved me and Burnie, I mean he *truly* loved us. It's amazing to think now that he had the ability to love so deeply as a parent when he had never been loved as a child.

The day that certified letter came in the mail to my Mother, my life changed forever. I remember thinking to myself how awful it was to break up with a woman in the same way that he wooed her. The same man who wrote her love letters back in those early years in Alabama, was the same man that wrote those kind and generous and beautiful words to express his love for my Mother. He used the same hand that addressed that letter. The same eyes that looked over to her in that small church when they first met, were the same eyes that were cast down when he saw her at the kitchen table after Burnie's death. The same lips that kissed her on their wedding day were the same lips that kissed her cheek as she wept over the death of their daughter. The hands that painted those forest green walls and white molding, were the same hands that opened the door when the furniture was being moved from Pittsburgh to California.

The relationship that I had with my father was complicated. I don't think children ever get over the divorce of their parents. I think it's just simply too much to bear. For me and Burnie, my Father not only divorced my Mother, but he divorced us too. He felt so bad for what he did. I always say that shame is a powerful drug. It cripples you and can cause you to do things that you never thought you would do. My Father was paralyzed with shame, and he couldn't bring himself to communicate with Burnie and me because he knew he would have to go through my Mother.

I forgave my Father long ago for how he broke up with our family and how he allowed the relationship that he had with my Mother to tarnish the relationship he would not have with Burnie and me. I forgave him for having another woman and family live in our beloved family home. Everyone who knows me knows that I speak highly of my Mother. Rarely do I speak of my Father. I think it's because I didn't know him well. I knew what I wanted him to be, what I desired for him to be, what I longed for him to be, but the truth of the matter is that I didn't know him. As a teen and throughout my childhood he shared stories with me about his life, but I didn't know his heart. It must have been hard for him to watch us grow up in a world so foreign to him and his experiences. How painful it must have been to see us carefree enjoying a life that he could've never imagined. I'm sure, as he stood watch at those parties and as we grew into our womanhood, he would watch at a distance imagining what it must have felt like to be loved and cared for by parents. I wonder what his life would have been like had his mother lived long enough to raise him, and his father love him instead of work him so hard. I wonder if he lived with regret. I wonder if he lived with sadness. I wonder if he ever spoke of it to my Mother. I wonder if secretly, he too was a wounded child who just wanted to be unconditionally loved by somebody, anybody. I wonder if that's why it was so easy for him to leave my Mother. His mother had died and left him when he was so young, all he knew was loss and abandonment. I wonder if it was easy for him to cut our family off because his family had cut him off emotionally. I wonder. It's interesting to me that people go through things in their lives, and we think that they're just bad people or they've made bad choices. We rarely consider what has happened to them to cause them to make poor choices, and then be defined as bad people. Perhaps, that's the greatest lesson of all, to know one's own story. When you know and then share your story you can empathize with others. That's what we should do. Telling your story could be the very thing that saves a life or changes a mind. I wish I knew the totality of my Father's story. I wish I could tap into the innermost parts of him to see his pain and his heart. I know some of his experiences, but I wish I could get into the soul of how he felt and what his needs and wants were. Men don't talk about such things and I never thought to ask.

My prayer is that my Father found peace after the divorce. My prayer is that he was able to forgive himself as he lay awake looking at those forest green walls. My prayer is that he was visited upon by his Mother to remind him to do things differently than what was done to him. Whether those things ever happened or not, in my mind, I think that's what would have saved my Father from a life of regret.

Decades had passed since my Father and I saw each other. After the divorce, he continued living in the Lewis Estate. It always bothered me that he lived there. He never really wanted to buy the house in the first place, yet he enjoyed living there for years. The forest green walls and white molding must have been a constant reminder of all that he had abandoned, all that he had lost. His was a sad life, void of family, connection, and his daughters. Burnie never made amends with him and I struggled to do so too. After the dust had settled and my life was getting back to the new normal without my Mother, I decided to reach out to my Father. During a particularly tense phone call, he informed me that he had married a woman named Hilda and that I had a stepsister, Vashti. Stepsister? **MY** sister was resting at Forest Lawn Cemetery in Hollywood Hills. I was taken aback. Married, again. **AND** a stepsister? . My Father had done it again, dropped a bombshell of information with little to no care or concern about how it would implode in my life. By no means was he obligated to appease me or protect my feelings, but he had divorced my Mother through the mail and now this.

I eventually met his wife, Hilda, and her daughter, Vashti. They were both pleasant and sweet. Hilda was a short, heavy woman with beautiful hair who was wheelchair bound. She was also 10 years his junior. She was meek and mild, certainly never challenging my Father. After spending a bit of time with her, I understood why she had been my Father's choice. She was nothing like my Mother. Her mild, almost submissive manner was reminiscent of my grandmother Joanna. She often commented about how she admired my drive and assertive nature. She was a peacemaker and went along with everything my Father said. He was finally free from the binds of his Father's tight grip and he wanted to make sure everything, including his relationships, were also free.

We had maintained a loving, open relationship for many years. I didn't talk to my Father daily or weekly, but I made the decision to always be there for him if he needed me. I needed to forgive him for the hurt he caused my Mother and our family. I needed to be present for him in a way that he had not been for me throughout my life. I could no longer hold the anger and pain in my heart because it would destroy me. I had to release it to God and allow my Father the freedom to live with his own choices. I, for one, wasn't going to continue punishing him for his poor decisions. Rather, I decided to do what Jesus does for me daily, forgive.

My Father had always been in good health. He didn't take medication and he was strong, even in his senior years. He loved hunting and would often go to the woods with his buddies to hunt deer and wild boar. I made sure that he was stocked with the very best rifles for his hunting trips. One morning, while he was retrieving one of those prized rifles, he tripped down the basement steps at the Lewis Estate, fell, and broke his neck. He died laying right there, in the bowels of our original family home. It was a sad day to learn that he had died. I wept and then did what I always have — work. I assisted Hilda with making all the arrangements. I had become an unfortunate expert in the matter of funeral preparation and the like. I arranged for my Father to be buried in Pittsburgh and there, we had a small, intimate service to celebrate his life. I was grateful that I had forgiven him years before. Standing over that casket all I could do was think about what could have been. I thought about the sheer joy of those trolley rides and how he would judge the sesame seed contests between me and Burnie at our family outings to Bob's Big Boy. I thought about how drawn he was when he knelt to kiss my Mother's cheek while she sat in the kitchen after Burnie died. I thought about my Daddy and how tragic his upbringing had been and how even as an old man, he was still gripped by his Father's rage. I reflected on the fact that he lived and died with a new wife, in a house that he never wanted my Mother to purchase. It was a sad life, but it didn't have to be so.

My Father was never able to live the true fullness of his life. He was embryonic with most of his dealings, including being a father.

He did what he thought was best, but he had left us long before he sent that certified letter to my Mother. He was a continuing victim of his Father's hardness and abuse. At the time of his death, I often wondered if he had any regrets. I wondered if he felt the weight of grief that I felt when he divorced our family. I was his daughter and his painting partner. We forged our relationship one brush stroke at a time. I realized that as we painted together covering old walls and radiators, we were also covering his wounds and what emerged was a new, fresh, open space to write more family history. Now, as an older woman, I know that covering up his past, much like repainting the many walls and doors, provide only temporary shelter from his reality. What we cover will eventually peek through the cracks and buckles that we try to hide. That's what happened to my Dad. His past was always one thin layer of forest green paint away.

My Father and Hilda had been married over 40 years when he passed and soon after his services, I was informed that he had left me an inheritance. He left the exact same amount of money to both Hilda and me. When I received my check in the mail from the probate attorney, I promptly issued another check in the same amount from my personal account directly to Hilda. She deserved to have peace of mind and financial stability after my Father died. If he wasn't going to do right by her, I was going to make sure she was taken care of. No woman should ever have to rely on a man to survive or thrive. That was the legacy my Father taught my Mother and my Mother, in turn, taught me. I sent the check by **CERTIFIED MAIL**.

The Dr. La-Doris McClaney School of Performing Arts and Communications

On occasion I am rendered speechless. It doesn't happen often, but it does happen. I try to live my life in a manner where people know exactly who I am. I make no apologies for my opinions and at this stage of my life, I freely speak my truth. On those occasions where my tongue is bridled, I find myself feeling awkward and unsteady in my thoughts. I have never welcomed surprises and I don't enjoy a lot of pomp and circumstance. I would much rather celebrate others than be celebrated myself. With that being said, I was thrust into the forefront of a moment in time and there is no escaping the lasting and permanency of it all.

For decades I have been a dedicated supporter of HBCUs and the education of Black people. My contributions to the United Negro College Fund have sent several students to college and I continue to funnel money and resources into causes that uplift, inspire, and educate young Black people. Because of my affiliation with Bethune-Cookman University, I made a special individual contributions to the institution. In honor of Dr. Bethune and my Mother, I gave $1Million to the school. It was a small gesture compared to the impact that the alumni and student body have made on the Black community in Daytona Beach, Florida and around the world. As a Trustee, and now as a Trustee Emeritus, I have been able to serve in an academic and fiscal position to ensure that the legacy started by Dr. McCleod-Bethune would last for all time. Little did I know that in 2015, I was about to have my name and legacy intertwined with hers and this exceptional institution forever.

When God speaks, I move. It has always been like that with He and I. I do not procrastinate and try to figure out what He's saying or why He's saying it. I simply heed his instructions. In early 2015, I heard from God. I was a sitting Trustee at Bethune and I was enjoying my position of service there. While on hiatus from our duties, God instructed me to contact Dr. Edison Jackson, then president of Bethune-Cookman University. I sat in my home office unsure as to why God instructed me to call Dr. Jackson. When I was patched into his direct line, God told me to tell Dr. Jackson that I was going to pledge $1Million to the school. Period. That's all He said. There was no condition or explanation, just pledge the money and hang up the phone! Dr. Jackson was elated that I heeded God's instruction and said, "have a wonderful day, Dr. Jackson. Goodbye." Just then, I could hear my Mother in my spirit, "well done daughter." I wept. Months later, I arrived at the University for our scheduled Trustee meeting. When I entered the door and sat around our conference table, Dr. Jackson rose to his feet and said, "La-Doris, the Board has decided to name a building in your honor." Wait? What? A building was going to be named after me? I almost fell out of my chair. While sitting there, I thanked the Board for their consideration, but inside I was bursting into tears at the thought of such an honor. My Mother had *literally* planted a seedling here decades before and now, it had taken root and a building bearing our family name, sprang forth!

On a warm October day in 2015, surrounded by friends, family, faculty, Trustees, and students, I watched as the Dr. La-Doris McClaney School of Performing Arts and Communications was born. There it was, my name, on a building, on the college campus named after a woman that my Mother admired so deeply. Before that day, I had only seen my full name on deeds and bills! But there it was, on a beautiful brick building and it was going to be there for all time. Weeks before the unveiling, I hired an up-and-coming Black photographer, Will Utley, to come to my home and shoot the portrait that would hang in the building. He positioned me so that a bust of my Mother, that was gifted to me by a neighbor after my Mother's death, would appear right over my shoulder. After the naming ceremony had ended, I, along with my 50 guests and the body of supporters walked the halls of the building. There, in the foyer, hung my portrait with the bust of my Mother just behind my shoulder. I wept again. I am sure that she would have gotten a kick out of seeing our family name and her daughter's picture there. I thought about how she created this legacy and how she taught me how to give and to serve. I watched as my family took pictures of each brick and tile, our family name, and my portrait.

When the weight of the day began to settle in, we were ushered upstairs to a reception. I was serenaded by a gifted choir of students who sang Let Me Call You Sweetheart by Bing Crosby. I was asked to speak after the serenade, and I was overwhelmed with gratitude. I had no intention of giving to get a building in my name. I heeded the call and God did the rest. I learned in that season that listening to God is the greatest prize. Although the building is an honor, the true building that I await is the mansion that God has prepared for me in heaven. I am in no rush to get there because I know that He has more work for me to do here. In the meantime, before I meet Him in my mansion, I get to commune with him in a magnificent building, near a magnificent shade tree, on a magnificent campus, in Daytona Beach.

International Students at Home

My favorite cousin, Denise Hendrick Turner, who is the daughter of my uncle Tommie Lee, introduced me to the idea of hosting international students in my home. Denise has always kept in close contact with me since the passing of my sister, Mother, and Grannie. She made sure that I was doing well and assured me that she was always there for me. I'm so grateful for her kindness. At first, I was completely against the idea because I am a single woman who lives alone, and I like it that way. For so long, I had to share my life with so many people and in this season, I just wanted to be alone, so I was apprehensive. I had already been in the residential care business for over twenty-five years, and I no longer wanted to deal with jealous social workers, building and safety regulations, fire department inspections, and everything else that goes into that line of work. Once she explained the process and how it wasn't anything like my past experiences, I took a chance and entered another new world.

Denise contacted someone from Kaplan International School for Students, and a representative immediately came out to inspect my home. By the time she finished a tour of the house, she wanted to move in too. I wanted to give the students a home and show them that a Black woman could be a self-made millionairess through hard work, education, and pure grit. I wanted to show them that Black women are powerful and can be rich, giving, and fun-loving. I showed them that Black women are capable of anything. My first six students were from China. We had a lot to talk about because I had visited China on four different occasions. On one trip, I had attempted to climb the steps of the Great Wall, although that didn't turn out so well. I was amazed that all my students started calling me Mommy. They said I felt like a Mother to them. I was honored. I was becoming to them what my Mother was to the staff and residents at Flagstone all those years ago.

People often ask if I ever wanted biological children. Being a Black woman born in 1938 meant, for many, a path that began with graduation from high school, entering college, meeting the man of your dreams, getting married, having children, and settling into traditional family life. I certainly do not knock anyone who chose this way of living, on the contrary, I was a direct beneficiary of my Mother being this kind of woman. She was strong and fearless, and a great supporter of my Father and devoted Mother to me and Burnie. I watched her become everyone's mother at Lewis Estate and Flagstone and her love and nurturing ways extended far beyond the children that she bore. I would have welcomed motherhood with open arms, but it was never something I actively thought about or desired. Being single and childless has allowed me the freedom to serve and give in ways that may have been prohibitive had I taken a more traditional route. By no means have I abandoned and ignored my maternal instincts. My international students are my children. I have "nieces" and "nephews," children of my friends, who have provided me a tremendous amount of joy over the years and who have allowed me to be an important member of their village. I also learned that marriage wasn't a necessary facet in my life either. I was able to continue to build upon our family legacy without the aid of a husband, his resources, or his permission. I don't think that women should have to fit any traditional narrative just to appease society or the beliefs imbedded into our DNA about wifehood and motherhood. You must listen to what the Spirit says to you for YOUR life and then, respond accordingly. That is what I did, and it worked for me.

When I opened my home to my international students, I could have never believed that I would mother so many. My home is perfectly situated for housing students, as I only live one mile from UCLA. The students love living at McClaney Estate because it was not only extremely comfortable, but it is also convenient. They lived within walking distance from campus. Having students in my house turned it into a home again. My only regret is that I did not do this earlier in my healing process. My Mother would have loved having the students in the house. She would have barbecued and made sweet potato pies for them every day. I suspect that had they known her, they would have loved her too. The movement of people made my home sing. I opened my home to host students in 2013 until the pandemic hit in March 2020.

One of my students was an employee of the United Arab Emirates Royal Family. Ebrahim Shaaban Abdullah is from the Holy City of Makkah Al Mukarramah. He came as a student, staying with me for one year while he was studying for his master's degree at Pepperdine University, a private University in Malibu, California, and my alma mater. He worked for the Royal Family of the United Arab Emirates, H. H. Sheikh Sultan bin Khalifa Bin Zayed Al Nahyan, and while he stayed with me, two of the Royal grandsons, Sheikh Zayed and Sheikh Mohammed, visited us. It was my first experience having Royals from the Middle East visit my home. They invited me to visit Abu Dhabi, Al Ain City, and Dubai, and they hosted me at the Royal Palace. Never had I seen such opulence. Dubai felt like home. Hosting international students has been a new lifeline for me. I have enjoyed the interaction, visiting their countries, and learning about their culture. Most of the students that I host are physicians, students working on their master's degree, doctoral candidates, scientific researchers, or visiting professors. They have always been pleasant, focused on their goals, and they have been a joy in my life when I didn't think joy would ever return.

On several occasions, I was able to visit the Middle East with one of my best friends, Dorothy Ellis. We traveled on the luxurious Emirates Airlines. The sixteen-hour, nonstop flight to Dubai, was long, but the airline has every comfort of home at 30,000-feet in the air. We were able to meet some of the Royal Family. I also had a chance to reconnect with Juma Mohammed Sultan Al Kahili, a member of the Royal family, by marriage, who had stayed with me in Holmby Hills for a year. Juma lives in Al Ain City in the United Arab Emirates. We were treated like royalty when we were in Dubai. We were given a driver who took us anywhere, anytime. The shopping in Dubai is next level. We loved going in and out of the designer stores, picking up fabulous fashions along the way. We visited every shop in the city. Our driver would carry our bags and was our personal assistant and concierge around the clock. I wore my Abaya most of the time. I loved the experience because I didn't have to do my hair or my makeup. Some of the ladies in the mall would speak to me in Arabic even though I didn't understand what they were saying. I blended in beautifully in Dubai. It was just fantastic.

Juma took us to his large camel farm. I was scared to death when I saw the camel open his mouth. I never knew camels were such gentle creatures though. Their tongues were as long as my leg. Who knew? Juma said that the camels were a little nervous because they had never seen a woman at the farm. We stayed for two weeks and visited again the following year for another two weeks. The architecture was so impressive and the real gold embellishments were endless. They were as impressive as the forest green walls and Gilbert's Fine Furniture from the Lewis Estate. I had never been around such lavish décor in my life. It was hard to keep my mouth closed. When visiting Juma's home, his Father invited us to come back for dinner the following day where they would kill a lamb in my honor. I was humbled by their gesture. It was the Alabama smokehouse and community feeding all over again.

Visiting the Palace was an experience in and of itself. Looking at the guards standing at the gates with guns in their hands was a little unnerving. I looked at Dorothy and said, "Do you think we will get out of here alive?" She smiled and said, "I hope so." During the lunch break, we were asked to join the Royal Table. This was considered a high honor. Picky me found a few things to eat, but Dorothy ate her heart out. I'm sure my Mother was looking down on us with a smile on her face, wishing she was there eating and likely slicing a sweet potato pie to serve for dessert.

The McClaney Estate in Holmby Hills Today

McClaney Estate, my home, sits on approximately one acre. The house was built in 1948 by one of the most famous Black architects, Paul Williams. Mr. Williams built homes in areas that he was unable to live in at the time. While drawing his designs, he would sit on the opposite side of the table fearful that a White woman would claim that he touched her. My home is a two-story 7,129-square-foot house consisting of a large entry hall, with a beautiful iron and crystal chandelier, living room, music room, bar, library, formal dining room, breakfast room, kitchen, butler's pantry, two bedrooms with one bath, and a powder room. Outside the living room are large ceiling-to-floor windows with a beautiful view of a waterfall and lush garden. The scenery is breathtaking. There are over 250 mature trees on the property. There are rose gardens and many secluded areas for peace and quiet. The second floor has two master suites each with their own private bathrooms, steam showers, and private balconies. It also boasts three additional bedrooms and two bathrooms upstairs. Separating the main house from the guest house is a large crescent shaped driveway. The private guest house overlooks the nearly Olympic-sized swimming pool, nestled within beautiful greenery and trees. The guest house has a large bedroom, two bathrooms, and a kitchen with a washer and dryer. At night when the grounds are illuminated, you feel as though you are in another world. It is majestic and tranquil. We were the first Black family to move into Holmby Hills. My home sits behind ten-foot high electric gates making it completely secluded. I have interior and exterior cameras to patrol my grounds to ensure my safety and security.

In 2006, I decided that I wanted to add on to my house. I wasn't interested in buying another house, but I wanted to create a master suite for myself. I hired an architect and told him what I wanted, and he drew up the plans. I looked into the Apartment Owner's Association book and I said, "Oh God, let my fingers stop at the right contractor." After interviewing many companies, I selected a Korean construction company to do the work. I asked a friend of mine, Lemar McNair, if he would oversee the project because he is an engineer and had experience with large-scale construction. I didn't know the difference between maple or oak wood, so I trusted Lemar to assist me in choosing the finishes for the addition. I pulled my own permits in my name only. I felt if anything went wrong, I would have full control over the construction project. Lemar did an exceptional job and would inform me when it was time to make payment.

I demolished the existing three-car garage and created an 1,800-square-foot garage in its place. I can now park nine cars inside if I desire. I use the garage as a ballroom when I want to entertain my guests, especially during my annual Christmas parties. Above the garage, I built an 1,800-square-foot master bedroom featuring a bathroom that has a shower with a floor-to-ceiling waterfall. The project turned out breathtaking. I beamed with pride having had the vision of the addition designed without compromising the integrity of the original home created by Mr. Williams, afterall, he is the same architect that designed the Beverly Hills Hotel, Neiman Marcus in Beverly Hills, The Brown Derby, Encounter at Los Angeles International Airport, and the list goes on. Later, I added an elevator, installed a small kitchen, and laundry room. This allows me to enter my home and go directly upstairs without any interference.

In 2014, at my Annual Christmas Party, I was never more surprised when I was asked to stand with Lady Mae Blake, Janice Smallwood McKenzie, and Jackie Castillo. I couldn't imagine what they wanted.

They announced to me and all of my guests that I was going to be honored by the City of Los Angeles City Council on January 16, 2015 declaring it Dr. La-Doris McClaney Day in the City. I was so shocked! What an honor. At that time, I think I was the only Black woman that had been bestowed such an honor. The morning of the ceremony, Tommy and I, along with all of my international students traveled to Los Angeles City Hall. I was shocked once again when I entered the council chambers. It was standing room only. This honor was also placed in the Library of Congress by Congresswoman Karen Bass. After the ceremony, we were escorted upstairs for a lunch reception. Oh, what a day.

As of March 2020, America and the world were in the throes of a pandemic. Many businesses closed because of Covid-19. To date, over half a million Americans have died due to the virus. I decided that this would be a good time for me to write my life story since I was housebound with plenty of time to reflect on my life. Amr and Wadie insisted that I write my book myself because no one knows my story better than me.

Quarantine afforded me plenty of time to commit to writing since I stayed home and honored the guidelines of the health officials. I maintained my distance from others, constantly washed my hands, and always wore a mask while I was outside of my home. I was very careful. I have been fully vaccinated and pray that I will not be affected by this brutal virus in the future. 2020 was a bitter and sweet year. I watched as the first African American and Southeast Asian woman, and my Link sister, Kamala Harris, was sworn in as Vice President of the United States of America. With pride and determination, a new generation of Freedom Fighters, from all over the world, protested the brutalization of Black people at the hands of rogue police officers. And now, in writing, I leave a legacy.

God really has been good to me and I am grateful for His mercy. I thank God that I have been able to remember as much as I have. Even with the ups and downs, I have lived a privileged life. I cannot and will not complain. I realize that I've lived longer than I will live. I don't fear death, rather, I celebrate life. Not just my past, but I celebrate my present and my future. I have lived a wonderful life. I've had beautiful relationships, nurturing parents, a loving sister, countless friends, and my faithful dogs. Throughout the years, my puppies, Angel, Amber, Woo, and Dewey have sustained me in ways that most humans could not. Dogs give unconditional love and though I've had many, the four that are I my life now are my favorites. The one Westie and three Scottish Terriers are ever loyal and ever loving. They follow me around like ducklings to a mother duck and in those moments when I'm quiet they know just when to nuzzle their wet noses near my hand for the appropriate belly rub. I never had children of my own, but my fur babies are my babies. I thank God for the life that I've had, and I look forward to all the things that He has next for me. God is still good and as I enter the golden days of my life and bask in the glow of the Son, my ear is still tuned to His voice and I remember that *God, I Listened Too*.

EPILOGUE

Precious La-Doris,

In self-publishing the autobiography of her beloved Mother Dr. Eula McClaney, *God, I Listened,* Dr. La-Doris McClaney presented to us the remarkable journey of an incredible woman. This priceless act of love in commemoration of her cherished Mother and extended to us, her readers, was a magnificent offering. Were it possible for most individuals to accomplish a feat of this magnitude, it would undoubtedly be the paragon achievement of their endeavors. But in the greatness of spirit, generosity of heart, and strength of character personified in the lives of Dr. Eula McClaney, Burnistine McClaney and Dr. La-Doris McClaney, our dear sister, La-Doris has surpassed the benchmark by magnanimously inviting us to again join her as she now recounts her own phenomenal journey, *God, I Listened Too.*

The fact that her story is not one of inherited wealth, inevitably multiplied with time and the manipulations of hired financial experts, nor is it the tale of a series of happy serendipitous coincidences, which buoyed and spread her speedily and effortlessly to a calm harbor of opulence, allows us to grasp the breadth and depth of her odyssey. In reading, we gained the invaluable benefit of her experience, hard won knowledge, skill, insight, and creativity. This candid account of an exceptional woman who as a young girl along with her sister traveled every step of a challenging journey shoulder to shoulder alongside her spirit led Mother striving and thriving despite the aggressive and hostile forces of poverty, racism and sexism, is an inspiring lesson in

195

the strength of family unity and the reward of valiant fearlessness. This narrative telling of three women who walked together the hard-uphill path with discipline, sacrificed strategy, and tremendous effort, with unfailing courage, dedication, and an unceasing wholehearted generosity, is an invaluable teaching on commitment and persistence. The chronicle of this stalwart woman who, when faced with first the devastating passing of her treasured sister followed closely by the passing of her irreplaceable Mother, did not falter but continue to march forward, is indeed a master class of perseverance, grace, and endurance despite overwhelming pain and loss.

Dr. McClaney has here unselfishly shared the treasure of her life, sowing seeds of inspiration, hope, navigational knowledge, and encouragement into the lives of her readers. Consequently, it follows that the trajectory of our journeys is positively affected thus exponentially increasing the impact of the gift of her story.

The sharing of her life in this way, is a bestowal that is most precious, but it comes as no surprise to us. For many years, we have watched as Dr. McClaney has walked with intention deftly weaving threads of love, faith, focus, fortitude, integrity, tenacity, and generosity into every fold of the tapestry of her life. It is fitting that remarkable success, charismatic significance, and powerful influence are hallmarks of her life. We have been grateful recipients; our lives enriched and enhanced greatly benefiting from her warm loving presence and friendship. It is our joy, that she has been both a friend and faithful member of West Angeles Cathedral for well over 25 years. Her wisdom, leadership, and generosity have been impactful in our lives and the ministry and life of West Angeles Cathedral. She has faithfully worked and supported West Angeles in its evangelical and charitable endeavors here in the United States and across the globe.

Dr. La-Doris McClaney is a wonderful woman of grace, dignity, class, stature, strength, sophistication, and elegance. Yet all these amazing attributes and qualities, while shining brightly, are eclipsed by her graceful humility and deep fervent love for God and his people.

It is with great joy and anticipation that we now look forward to the next chapters of the life of Dr. La-Doris McClaney. Doubtless, the close of this book is not an ending, but instead an auspicious new beginning for a journey toward future triumphs and accomplishments. She however, will not travel forward alone because we beneficiaries have been inspired, entertained, and strengthened, by this offering of *God, I Listened Too* will each continue to move forward also helping one another as we step boldly and joyfully with this eloquent reminder that with faith, inextricable bound of wisdom, dedication and work, nothing is impossible. This clarion call and promise, dear readers, is indeed the Legacy of this wonderful incomparable woman, our dear sister Dr. La-Doris McClaney.

Presiding Bishop Charles E. Blake, Sr., and Lady Mae L. Blake
International Churches of God in Christ, Inc.
West Angeles Cathedral, Church of God in Christ,
Los Angeles, California

A Message

to Bishop Charles E. Blake, Sr., and Lady Mae L. Blake

For over 30 years, I have found myself in a place of gratitude. Not that I had been ungrateful in the past, but I now think upon the blessings of God in a very deliberate and purposeful way. For many years following the deaths of my Mother and Burnie, I didn't think that I would ever know joy or peace or be grateful for anything. I've said on several occasions that I would give up every worldly possession in an instant just to see the faces of my Mother and Burnie again. I long to hear the laughter that could cause the walls to shake with deafening joy. In those years, I lived in a fog of despair and a swirling vortex of frustration with God and how He could forsake me by taking my dear Mother, sister, grandmother, and even my Father. My anger and sadness nearly destroyed me. I was broken and couldn't find my way out of the hole that had been dug for me by the shovel of death and loss. I didn't want to die, I just didn't know how to live. By 1990, I had a change of view and heart. I decided that I wanted to live life to the fullest on my own terms, and that's exactly what I did.

I had always been taught that if you find yourself in a position of despair, you must look up to the hills to find strength. As it is written in the Bible, in Psalm 121, *"I will lift up mine eyes unto the hills, from whence cometh my help. My help cometh from the Lord."* Though my gaze was cloudy, and I was unable to see the God in my life, I knew where to find help. Even with the ability to buy whatever I wanted and wanting for nothing, nothing could ever fill the void of my loss. When a loved one dies, people cope with it in many ways. I went inward. I was having parties and celebrating accomplishments and living a privileged life, but something was missing. Where was my help? I discovered it on a Sunday morning in Los Angeles where I found myself walking into the sanctuary at West Angeles Church of God in Christ. I stepped into the doors of the church looking for a space to disappear in my grief and was met with a bright light of love that forbade me from sitting in darkness, but rather commanded me to bask in the blinding Glory of the Almighty. I knew I was home. I was embraced with the open, loving arms of Bishop Charles E. Blake, Sr., and Lady Mae L. Blake, and sailed into service to God and His people.

As shepherds, they guided me into the presence of God and taught me how to worship Him more deeply and faithfully. I have always had a relationship with my Savior, but Bishop Blake ushered me into a deeper, more intimate space with God. In I Timothy 3:2, the Bible says that *"an overseer has to be temperate, respectable, above reproach, self-controlled, able to teach and, most importantly, faithful to his wife."* A similar sentiment is supported in a pastor's duties to the church, as outlined in the Book of Acts. Plainly, Acts 20:17-32 states that *"a pastor must preach the Word of God in its entirety without holding anything back. They must be a good example for their church. They should be dedicated to their people and be invested in their lives."* My experiences with Bishop Blake and Lady Mae have demonstrated their commitment to their responsibilities as the shepherds of the flock of West Angeles Cathedral. I am fully aware of my own shortcomings and deficiencies, but my church family has allowed me to become my full self and express myself in a way that truly honors God and the legacy of my family.

I thank them for their outpouring of support and love and wish only to continue my work expanding the Kingdom of God in a way that is pleasing to Him. They saved my life. Their love and prayers sustained me when nothing else would fill my empty cup that now runneth over. I am eternally grateful to them. I will always love them.

My prayer is that each and every person that I have touched sees the power and Sovereignty of God at work. I am now truly and fully living my **BEST** life and it is because of Him that I am! I faithfully and continually attune my ear to His voice, that's why, God, I Listened Too.

Dr. La-Doris McClaney

WISDOM OF THE DAY

Wisdom 1:

It is painful and hurtful but always remember whatever you have gone through, someone else has gone through the same thing. It is not what you go through, it is about how you handle these situations. Your strength must come from deep faith in God and perseverance. Now, today as I look back, I could have been in Africa or lived somewhere else - who knows, but God had something else planned for me.

Wisdom 2:

Things will always come to you on time and in time. If they come to you in a hardship, on the other side, there is a rainbow. You need sunshine and water to make a rainbow. It takes both. You must have faith. With Him guiding you, nothing is impossible. We lived in a place with no electricity or plumbing and if we hadn't believed, we would not have ended up here in Holmby Hills.

Wisdom 3:

What you do when you are young will reflect on you when you grow old. Patterns and pathology are real. My Mother was taking in foster children when I was a young girl, and I took in foster children as young adult and as a senior adult today, I am taking in international students. I had inspiration from my Mother when I was young and continued this as an adult.

Wisdom 4:

I have found that no matter how high you go, economically, publicly, emotionally, death can make you feel that you'll give it all up to have your loved one back. Remember, things are not important, it is the love that you have from heart to heart and breast to breast that is important. People tend to worship the wrong things. What matters is the love that you have for your family and others.

Wisdom 5:

Never feel that you are better than anyone else. We are one of the same. This pandemic has taught us a lot. It does not matter if you are a king or a servant, actor, or athlete, we are all in the same boat. Large companies are crumbling under the weight of a tiny, yet powerful virus today. One of the most prestigious stores, *Neiman Marcus* in Beverly Hills is now in bankruptcy. Forty percent of the stores located on world-renowned Rodeo Drive are closed.

Wisdom 6:

Never desire to be anyone other than yourself. You are perfect in the image that the almighty God made you. You may look at other people and say I wish I were this person or that person. You envy the result but rarely see the work. If someone gives you the same roadmap and say that you must go through the same things that person you are admiring has gone through, you may not be willing to take the same road. So never desire to be someone else other than who you are. However, if you want to change your situation, the only person who can navigate that and do that is you. You must work for what you want to get in this life.

Wisdom 7:

Always remember all man's evil never outweighs God's good. When you are a good person and do the right thing, God will always protect you and take care of you. I learned this lesson through my haters, employees, marriage and throughout my life. God will never let you down.

AWARDS AND HONORS

2020 – Received an Appreciation Award for generous contribution to the Vision 2020 Campaign.

October 2019 – Recipient of the President's Award, Green & White Gala, Beverly Hills West (CA) Chapter of The Links, Incorporated, Los Angeles, California.

February 2017 - Recipient of the Certificate of Recognition by the California State Legislature, Office of the Speaker, Sacramento, California.

February 2017 - Unveiling of the McClaney Family Resource Center by Los Angeles County Board of Supervisors, Supervisor and Board Chairman Mark Ridley-Thomas, 2nd District, Los Angeles, California.

February 2017 - Certificate of Recognition issued by the California State Assembly and the 63rd Assembly District, Anthony Rendon, Ph.D. Speaker of the Assembly in gratitude for the support of the South-Central Los Angeles Regional Center.

January 2017 - California Senate Resolution Recognition Award. The Assembly honors Dr. La-Doris McClaney for her personal and professional achievements, her strong support of the community and her exemplary record of public service. This is the highest commendation issued by the people of California. Presented by Kevin de Leon, President of California Senate Assembly, Sacramento, California.

July 2016 – Entrance into the 1946 Society, at The Links Foundation, Inc. 40th National Assembly, Las Vegas, Nevada.

October 2015 – Recipient of a Certificate of Appreciation from Fellowship West, Inc. and became a Member of the National Rehabilitation Association.

April 2015 – Recipient of the Brother's Keeper Award and Ambassador of Goodwill Shining Light of Life at the 12th African Goodwill Recognition Award Ceremony at the Concourse Hotel LAX, Los Angeles, California.

January 2015 – Recognition of career achievements by The Links, Incorporated presented by Glenda Newell-Harris, MD, 16th National President.

January 2015 – Statement of Congratulations on Dr. La-Doris McClaney Day for "enriching lives" by the Los Angeles County Board of Supervisors, Supervisor Mark Ridley-Thomas, 2nd District, Los Angeles, California.

January 2015 – Recognition of Dr. La-Doris McClaney Day in the City of Los Angeles, and placement into the congressional record, by the Honorable Karen Bass, United States House of Representatives, during the Proceedings and Debates of the 114th Congress, First Session, Washington, D.C.

2015 – Inducted into the Dr. Richard V. Moore Legacy Society at Bethune-Cookman University, Daytona Beach, Florida.

2008 – Woman of Achievement from Lupus LA, Los Angeles, California.

2005 – Recipient of the Business Foundation Award in appreciation for tireless support of the law enforcement community, by AFSCME, Deputy Probation Officers Union, Local 685, Los Angeles, California.

1998 – Recipient of a Certificate of Appreciation for outstanding and dedicated service 13-94/3-7 to the Board Of Directors of Charles R. Drew University of Medicine and Science.

October 1996 – Recipient of the 5th Annual Living Legends Award presented for outstanding leadership and service.

April 1995 – Recipient of the Status of Women Award for meritorious service as a Philosophic Entrepreneur, presented by the Top Ladies of Distinction, Inc., Lady Nina Alexander, President.

May 1992– National Coalition of 100 Black Women for outstanding women in business, Virgina.

October 1992 – Recipient of the Honorary Humanitarian Award for her outstanding contribution to Higher Education presented by B.I.A.P.A., Inc., Marlene Dove, Founder and dedicates the Eula McClaney Performing Arts Center in Memory of La-Doris' beloved Mother.

October 1991 – Recipient of an Award of Appreciation for her role as guest speaker for the Homewood-Brushton Community Improvement Association, Inc., (HBCIA), presented by Carrie L. Wynn, President and Ruby Hord, Executive Director, Pittsburgh, Pennsylvania.

February 1991 – Recipient of the Appreciation Award for Exemplary Christian Service to the St. Paul A.M.E. Church, presented by Rev. V. Williams. Pastor.

February 1991 – Recipient of the Greetings Award proclaiming an
honorary citizenship of Bogalusa, Louisiana.

February 1991 - Recipient of an Appreciation Award for participa-
tion in the Authors Afternoon by the Our Authors Study Club,
The Los Angeles Branch of the National Association for the Study
of Afro-American Life and History, Los Angeles, California.

1991 – Recipient of the Presidential Award for Outstanding Achievement in Community Service presented by the Walter R. Tucker
Foundation, serving the Youth of Today - Leaders of Tomorrow.

1991 - Recipient of an Appreciation Award for dedicated service
on the Board of Directors from 1987 to 1991, presented by Daniel
Freeman Hospitals Foundation, Los Angeles, California.

October 1990 – Recipient of a Letter of Appreciation for her speech
of wisdom to the Business and Professional Auxiliary, West Angeles
Church of God in Christ, presented by Bishop Charles E. Blake.

August 1990 - Recipient of a Commendation by the Louisiana State
Senate, approved by a motion made by the Honorable Cleo Fields
for the debut of her book, *God, I Listened* and for her inspirational
devotion to serving her God by enthusiastically and energetically
caring about and sharing with her fellow man, presented by the
President of the Senate, State of Louisiana.

July 1990 – Recipient of the Women of First AME Church for
outstanding and dedicated service presented by Dr. W. Bartalette
Finney, Minister, Los Angeles, California

February 1990 - Recipient of a Certificate of Acknowledgement for her noteworthy contribution to the Los Angeles District Equal Employment Opportunity Program and for Serving to Further the Objectives of Equal Employment Opportunity, presented by the Department of the Treasury, Internal Revenue Service.

January 1990 – Recipient of the Drum Major Award for outstanding service and leadership to youth presented by the Youth Redirection Program of America.

1990 – Recipient of the Quality of Life Award presented by Sigma Gamma Rho Sorority, Inc., Sigma Sigma Chapter.

1990 – Recipient of a Service Award to the religious and literary communities, presented by the First African Methodist Episcopal Church, represented by Miffed Hawkins, Chairperson and Warren Campbell, Sr. Minister, Pasadena, California.

October 1989 - Recipient of a Certificate of Appreciation for serving as the mistress of ceremonies of the Inglewood-South Bay NAACP Eighth Annual Freedom Fund Awards Dinner, Viscount Hotel, Los Angeles, California.

1990 – National Coalition of 100 Black Women for outstanding women in business, New York City, New York.

September 1989 – Recipient of the First Annual Recycling Black Dollars Pioneer Award, presented at the Recycling Black Dollars Anniversary Dinner.

April 1989 - By the authority of the Board of Trustees of Bethune-Cookman University and upon the recommendation of the faculty, hereby confers upon La-Doris McClaney the degree Doctor of Humane Letters with all rights, honors, and privileges thereunto appertaining. In testimony whereof the seal of college and the signatures of its officers and hereunto affixed. Given at Daytona Beach, Florida, on April 24, 1989 by President of the College, Donald Bronson.

April 1989 – Recipient of the Act-So Award in grateful recognition for outstanding service, distinguished leadership, and dedicated enthusiasm to the community in the field of humanities and philanthropy presented by the NAACP West Coast Region, Los Angeles, California.

1989 – Recipient of the Samuel C. Berry Award for outstanding contributions to the Bethune-Cookman College Band Program.

1989 – Recipient of the Community Service Award, presented by the Kids Against Drug Campaign.

1988 – Recipient of an Appreciation Award in recognition of La-Doris McClaney for outstanding support in the fight against heart diseases, presented by the American Heart Association Greater Los Angeles affiliate.

December 1987 – Recipient of a Statement of Condolence, The State of California, by Governor George Deukmejian, Sacramento, California.

December 1987 - Received a Resolution in Memoriam from the California State Senate, Senator Diane E. Watson, 28th Senatorial District, Los Angeles, California.

December 1987 - Received a Resolution in Memoriam, California State Assembly, Assemblywoman Maxine Waters, 48th Assembly District, Los Angeles, California.

December 1987 - Received a Resolution of Sympathy and Remembrance, Bethune-Cookman University, Daytona Beach, Florida.

October 1987 – Recipient of the Woman of the Year Award, presented to Dr. La-Doris McClaney who was nominated by Neville and Neville, Public Relations in appreciation for her exceptional leadership qualities and integrity and her distinguished achievements for the betterment of her community, presented by the Centinela Business and Professional Women, Jill Olechno, President and March Fong Eu, Honorary Chair.

June 1987 – Commendation for Outstanding Achievement in Community Service and Philanthropy presented by Delta Sigma Theta Sorority, Inc., Century City Alumnae Chapter, Los Angeles California.

June 1987 - Recipient of The Madame C. J. Walker Award for Enterprise, Involvement and Transformation of the Community, presented by Operation PUSH, Chicago, Illinois.

April 1987 – Proclamation of La-Doris McClaney Day, in the City of Los Angeles, in Recognition of Community and Charitable Contributions by Mayor Tom Bradley, Los Angeles, California.

February 1987 - Ambassador for Goodwill and Support of Higher Education for the Youth of America, presented by Oswald P. Bronson. Sr., President of Bethune-Cookman University. Daytona Beach, Florida. November 1986 – Received a Resolution in Honor of Outstanding Contributions to Eleven Local Charitable Organizations, presented by the City of Los Angeles, Los Angeles, California.

February 1987 – Recipient of the Ambassador Award in recognition of Goodwill and Support of Higher Education for the Youth of America, Bethune-Cookman University, Daytona Beach, Florida.

1987 – Recipient of and award for outstanding contribution to the Sickle Cell Disease Research Foundation during their 30th Anniversary Celebration Gala.

1987 - Recipient of an Honorary Doctorate of Humanities, Shorter College, Little Rock, Arkansas.

November 1986 – Featured in an article in the Los Angeles Times and honored at a reception at Los Angeles City Hall, Los Angeles, California.

June 1986 – Received a Resolution in Honor of Dr. La-Doris McClaney from the Board of Trustees of Compton Community College, Compton, California.

June 1986 – Recipient of an Award for Unselfish Giving and Support in The Fight Against Lung Cancer, presented by The American Lung Association, Los Angeles, California.

June 1986 - Recipient of an award for Outstanding Achievement presented by the City of Compton, Mayor Walter Tucker, Compton, California.

June 1986 – Recipient of an award for Interest and Support of Cardiovascular Research and Community Education Programs presented by The American Heart Association, Los Angeles, California.

June 1986 - Recipient of the Meritorious Service Award presented by The United Negro College Fund, Los Angeles, California.

June 1986 – Recipient of an Award for Generous Contributions and Dedicated Service, presented by the Sickle Cell Research Foundation, Los Angeles, California.

June 1986 – Recipient of an Appreciation Award for Kindness and Generosity, presented by the American Diabetes Association, Los Angeles, California.

June 1986 – Recipient of an Appreciation for Generosity, presented by King/Drew School of Medicine, Los Angeles, California.

June 1986 - Recipient of the Presidential Humanitarian Award for sharing the goal of improving the quality of life for Blacks and other minorities, presented by the 100 Black Men of Los Angeles, Inc., Fred A. Calloway, President.

February 1986 – Recipient of a Certificate for Outstanding Achievement in Entrepreneurship, Entrepreneur Magazine, Los Angeles, California.

1986 – Recipient of an Award of Appreciation for love and support of the students of Alpha Schools.

1986 – Recipient of the Woman of the Year Award presented by the Sickle Cell Disease Research Foundation, Los Angeles Chapter, Los Angeles, California.

November 1984 - The Shaw University Citation of Appreciation, presented to Eula McClaney, Mother and distinguished friend of the University, Burnistine and La-Doris McClaney, distinguished Alumnae of the University, in recognition of their loyal and inspirational leadership, sacrificial service and spirit of cooperation in providing for the university's ongoing growth and development, presented by Dr. Stanley H. Smith, University President.

March 1984 – Recipient of a Commendation for Outstanding Community Service presented by the California State Legislature, Assemblywoman Maxine Water, 48th Assembly District, Sacramento, California.

March 1983 – Recipient of the Humanitarian of the Year Award, Los Angeles County Board of Supervisors, Los Angeles, California.

September 1981 – Received a Resolution for Outstanding Philanthropic and Humanitarian Endeavors presented by the State of Michigan, Detroit, Michigan.

September 1981 – Received a Proclamation from the City of Detroit, Mayor Coleman A. Young, Detroit, Michigan.

September 1981 – Recipient of the Entrepreneur, Philanthropist and Humanitarian Award presented by the Afro-American Museum of Detroit, Detroit, Michigan.

July 1981 – Recipient of a Certificate of Appreciation in Recognition of Induction into the Schomburg Center for Research and Black Culture, The Afro-American Newspaper, New York, New York.

June 1981 - Recipient of the Service To Youth Award, Weingart Urban Center YMCA, Los Angeles, California.

1981 – Recipient of the Award for Outstanding Contribution in the Field of Rehabilitation Southern California Rehabilitation Association, Los Angeles, California.

May 1979 – Recipient of an Achievement Award for Outstanding Community Service presented by the Women's Council, Consolidated Realty Board, Los Angeles, California.

1979 – Received a Certificate of Significant Achievement and Contribution from the State of California in Developing Economic Independence Among Young Adults, presented by the United States Senate, Senator S. I. Hayakawa, Los Angeles, California.

November 1978 – Received Recognition for Inspiration and Example to Others, United States House of Representatives, United States Congress, Washington, D.C.

October 1978 – Recognized as an Outstanding Citizen of Los Angeles by the Los Angeles City Council, Los Angeles, California.

October 1978 – Recipient of the Award of Merit for Outstanding Achievement in Service to the Developmentally Disabled, South Central Los Angeles Regional Center, Los Angeles, California.

October 1978 – Received a Certificate of Tribute for Outstanding Citizenship and Activities, Enhancing Community Betterment, City of Los Angeles.

August 1978 – Received a Resolution in honor of Personal and Professional Achievements from the California State Legislature, Los Angeles, California.

May 1978 – Recipient of a Certificate of Award for Outstanding Community Services presented by the Southwest Wave Newspaper, Los Angeles, California.

December 1975 - The Trustees of Pepperdine University on the recommendation of the Faculty of the Graduate School and by virtue of the authority in them vested have conferred upon La-Doris McClaney, the degree of Master of Public Administration, with all the rights, privileges and honors thereunto appertaining, Los Angeles, California.

December 1974 - Recipient of a Certificate of Achievement for excellence in outstanding adult care facility management presented by Exceptional Adult Center School, Los Angeles, California.

December 1974 – Received a Certificate of Achievement for High Standards of Excellence in the Management of a Family Care Facility, Exceptional Adult Center, Los Angeles, California.

1974 - Bachelor of Arts Degree, Shaw University, Raleigh, North Carolina.

October 1973 – Received a Certificate of Appreciation from the Los Angeles Junior Chamber of Commerce, Los Angeles, California.

August 1973 – By the authority of the Board of Trustees of Shaw University in Raleigh, North Carolina certifies that La-Doris McClaney has successfully satisfied all the academic and functional requirements for the Bachelor of Science Degree in Behavioral Science on August 20, 1973. Presented by Abdul h. Elkurdy, LED, MA, JD, PhD, Professor/Associate Dean and Robert Powell, Dean.

July 1973 – Recipient of a Certificate certifying that La-Doris McClaney was a registered participant in Management of Developmentally Disabled in Board and Care Homes presented by the University of California, Los Angeles, School of Public Health University Extension, Lester Bryton, Dean, School of Public Health.

1973 – Recipient of the YMCA Outstanding Service Award, Southside Los Angeles Century Club, Los Angeles, California.

Recipient of an Appreciation Award for deep friendship and generous support of service to young people by Young Men's Christian Association.

Recipient of the Business Achiever Award presented by the International Black M.B.A. Student Association.

Recipient of an Appreciation Award for kindness and generosity to the American Diabetes Association, and commitment to improve the lives of countless people with diabetes, presented by John Mace, MD, President of the American Diabetes Association, Southern California Affiliate.

Recipient of the Award of Recognition from the Bethune-Cookman University Concert Chorale for her generous contribution and devotion to Bethune-Cookman University, presented by Dr. Rebecca A. Steele, directress, and Gerald B. Yancey, Student Government Association President and Oswald P. Bronson, University President, Daytona Beach, Florida.

Recipient of the Commendation Award in recognition of dedicated service to the affairs of the community and for the civic pride demonstrated by numerous contributions for the benefit of all the citizens of Los Angeles County presented by the Beverly Hills West (CA) Chapter of The Links, Incorporated for A Jazz Odyssey Charity and Scholarship Benefit, Los Angeles, California.

Recipient of the Outstanding Service Award presented by The Links, Incorporated.

Became a member of the Los Angeles Chamber of Commerce.

Recipient of the National Rehabilitation Association Award for being committed to the enhancement of lives of persons with disabilities presented by Executive Director David L. Mills, Los Angeles, California.

Award of Recognition presented to Dr. La-Doris McClaney in appreciation of unwavering love and financial support of Bethune-Cookman University, presented by Dr. Edison O. Jackson, University President and Joe Petrock, Chairman of the Board of Trustees, Daytona Beach, Florida.

Renaming the School of Performing Arts as Dr. La-Doris McClaney School of Performing Arts and Communication. Bethune-Cookman University, Daytona Beach, Florida.

Recipient of a Commendation for Outstanding and Dedicated Efforts in Sickle Cell Disease Research, from the Los Angeles County Board of Supervisors, Los Angeles, California.

CPSIA information can be obtained
at www.ICGtesting.com
Printed in the USA
LVHW110710180721
692881LV00035B/670/J